MAKE MONEY FROM BLOGGING

BLOGGING

How To Start A Blog While Raising A Family

Lisa Tanner and Sally Miller

FREE BONUS

As a thank you for buying our book, we have created a bonus area to help you on your journey. The bonus area has a growing list of resources that will help you:

> Finally stop dreaming and start earning from home doing what you love.
> Discover the 7 steps to start a blog and earn $1000 (or more).
> Get a step-by-step guide that shows you exactly how to set up your blog (with zero technical skills and on a tiny budget).

Download your bonus resources here: sallyannmiller.com/bloggingbook

CONTENTS

INTRODUCTION

Sally Miller

Welcome and congratulations! By picking up this book, you've taken the first step to starting your blog. I don't know what inspired you to open these pages, but I can guess. Not so long ago, I was in your shoes. Learning everything I could about how to start a blog, create great content, and get my message out into the world.

I wanted more from life and I was hungry to learn. I uncovered plenty of information to feed my hunger, which is where I encountered my first problem. There's too much information online.

You can read about WordPress, Search Engine Optimization, email lists, content marketing, social media, affiliate marketing and more. It's all useful stuff. But where's the plan?

How do you know what to do first? What social media platforms are best? How often should you publish blog posts? How should you monetize your blog? How do you even get people to *read* your blog?

And of course, the greatest challenge of all:

How do you find time to get it all done?

Through research, taking courses, and lots of mistakes I unearthed answers to these questions. But I didn't do it alone. On my journey I had the help of some amazing colleagues and mentors. One of those people is my co-author, Lisa Tanner.

Before I met Lisa, I thought I was doing well managing my time. But Lisa takes things to a whole new level. She's a homeschooling mom to eight kids, a blogger, and a freelancer. Yup, you read that right. Lisa is raising eight kids while running a successful online business. What Lisa doesn't know about starting a blog and raising a family isn't worth knowing.

Something else I admire about Lisa is how intentional she is with her blog. It's tempting to hop from one project to the next. Chasing shiny objects. Trying the latest tactics. But when you have the demands of a large family, you don't have time to waste on ideas that don't work.

Lisa's approach to blogging is laser focused. She knows what she needs to do to publish amazing content and spread the word. And by the time you finish reading this book, you will too.

But let's rewind a bit. Maybe you're not sure whether you want to start a blog. I don't want you to waste your time with this book if it isn't the right path for you. So, let's look at what you need to be a successful blogger. I'll also discuss why you might want to start a blog in the first place.

WHO SHOULD START A BLOG?

First and foremost, you need to love writing. I'm going to be straight with you here. If you don't enjoy writing, forget about blogging. Go start a YouTube channel or Podcast instead. Because when you create a blog, you're going to be writing a lot.

I publish two articles a week. Each article is around 1,000 to 2,000 words. That's at least 3,000 words a week. On top of that, I publish several books a year. So, yes, I love writing. If I didn't, I'd have no chance of sustaining a blogging career.

Now, you don't have to be the best writer. I'm not. But by writing every week, you're going to improve faster than you thought possible. You just need to enjoy the process of turning your thoughts into words.

On its own, a love of writing isn't enough. You also need to be passionate about your blogging topic. You must have a subject or theme you love so much that you can write about it for a long time. Lisa dives deep into picking your niche in chapter one.

The good news is that you don't have to choose a narrow topic. It doesn't hurt to niche down, either. Writing about a single, well-defined subject makes it easy for others who share your passion to discover and read your blog.

However, I didn't niche down. I blog about working from home and living your best life. I'm multi-passionate—I love learning and sharing new ideas. On my blog, I cover a range of topics including self-publishing, freelancing, blogging, starting a coaching business, simple living, productivity, success, and work-life balance. Although I cover diverse topics, I have a common theme and a specific audience. My theme is profiting from work you love. And I write for stay-at-home parents who want more in their lives. Parents who want to stay home with their kids *and* earn an income—without feeling torn between the two.

Okay, you love writing and you've found something you're passionate about. What else do you need to be a successful blogger? Nothing. You're good to go!

You only need these two things to succeed. Everything else can be learned or outsourced. In fact, you will learn everything you need for your first year of blogging as you read this book.

WHY START A BLOG?

What can you reasonably expect after blogging for a year? Why even bother?

Let's talk about money first, because I know this is a pressing concern for most people. Here's what I want you to know. Despite what others might say, you *can* earn an income as a blogger. In this book, we share six ways to monetize your blog. After one year (assuming you're consistent and have a message people want to hear) you can earn anywhere from $1,000 a month to six figures a year.

In this book, we share the stories of six and even seven-figure bloggers. Yes, many of these people have been at it for a long time. But some started just one or two years ago. As you advance in your blogging career, you can grow a business around your blog. When you put your ideas out into the world, you make connections. You meet people who share your interests and new opportunities come your way.

Here are a few examples from my life. Through writing and blogging, I've been invited to speak at conferences, asked to coach people, and partnered with entrepreneurs who I once looked up to and never thought I'd get to know. You will be surprised at the doors that open once you start your blogging journey.

Which brings me to the most important reason to blog. It's not money. Or fame. Or connections. When you start blogging, you make a difference in people's lives. Your words impact others. You help your readers solve pressing problems and inspire them to reach for their dreams.

> As a blogger, you change people's lives. And that's powerful stuff.

When you receive emails from your readers thanking you because you helped them through a difficult time in their life, or a message describing how you gave them hope, that is the greatest reward of all.

START YOUR BLOGGING JOURNEY

Before you jump into the meat of this book, I have one last word of advice. Please take your time. Follow every step. And don't give up.

You're going to hit obstacles, technical challenges, fears and doubts. Things that don't work out as you hoped. It may take you months to figure out what you want to write about or who you're writing for.

That's okay. We all experience problems. It takes time to hone your writing voice and master the skills you need to be a successful blogger. Lisa and I have both encountered our share of obstacles. But the more you practice, the better you get as a writer, a blogger, and a businessperson. And the closer you'll come to creating a blog you and your readers love. A blog that brings in a consistent income—one you can fit around your family commitments.

> *Starting a blog can be overwhelming. But I don't want you to jump ship at the first obstacle. I've found that the solution to feeling overwhelmed is to have a plan.*

This book is your plan. And to make it even easier for you, I've created a bonus workbook. This downloadable workbook guides you through the steps to start your blog. It tells you exactly which chapter to read, what actions to take, and when to take them.

Also, when you download the workbook, you get email access to me. I'd love to support you on your journey. It's my mission to help other stay-at-home parents do work they love. If that sounds like something you want, hop over to the bonus area: sallyannmiller.com/bloggingbook. Then, turn to chapter one and start building your blog today.

Now, I hand you over to Lisa. Enjoy the book and I hope to meet you soon.

CHAPTER ONE

Create a Reader Persona

Are you ready to launch a money-making blog? I'm excited to help you on this journey and show you the ropes.

I've been around the blogosphere for several years now. I published my first blog posts in 2013. I learned a ton from that first blog and made loads of mistakes. It took me years to make any income from it.

But, I didn't give up. I started learning and experimenting. I invested in myself. And when I launched my second blog in 2015, I was ready. I've made a steady profit ever since then. In fact, in 2017, I averaged $2,300 a month.

What was different?

That's what you will discover as you read this book. I share all the nitty-gritty details I learned about using a blog to generate income. I want you to walk away with everything you need to start strong.

Of course, it takes time to get all the pieces in place. Blogging is *not* a get-rich-quick plan. However, if you follow the steps I present, you won't need to spend years trying to figure it out on your own.

Let's get started.

BUILD YOUR FOUNDATION

According to the Oxford English Dictionary, a foundation is "an underlying basis or principle for something." For a blogger, your foundation has two core components—who you're writing for and what you're writing about. In the rest of this chapter, I walk you through how to answer these two questions.

So, take the time now to think through your foundation-building process. Because if you don't get your foundation in place, your blog will have no clear direction and won't attract readers. Your readers are your potential customers. So, without readers, your chances of earning money from blogging will seriously diminish.

WHO IS YOUR BLOG FOR?

To make money from your blog, people must read it. Who will read your blog? Who are you writing for?

Don't say everybody. You cannot write content that appeals to everyone. It's not possible. There are millions of blogs online. If you try to attract everyone to yours, you will achieve the opposite.

No one will read it. They won't know why they should.

You must figure out who your ideal reader is. This is crucial, and it's a step I skipped with my first blog. I was writing for my family, but I also wanted to write about homesteading, homeschooling, and life in general.

I spent all my time writing for myself instead of for my readers. It's no wonder my blog didn't make any money for a long time.

I had no plan.

And as Benjamin Franklin said:

> *"If you fail to plan, you are planning to fail."*

Don't plan to fail. Keep reading to learn how to identify an ideal reader for your blog.

WHAT ARE YOU GOING TO BLOG ABOUT?

Before picking an ideal reader, you need to know what you want to blog about. This is your niche. Here are ten popular, money-making niches:

> Blogging/making money online
> Personal finance
> Health
> Survival
> College prep/higher education

> Tech

> Personal development

> Lifestyle

> Food

> Fashion

Are those the *only* niches you can pick to make money? No! There are plenty of bloggers making money in other niches, like Jennifer Maker. Her crafting blog now earns a full-time income. So, don't feel limited by this list of niches. They're just some of the most popular ones, not the only choices available.

What are you passionate about? As you create content for your blog, you will dedicate hours of your life every month to this topic. It's a lot easier if you pick something you know about and care about.

To help you find your niche, get out a piece of paper and a pen. Spend a couple of minutes brainstorming topics you would like to write about.

When you finish, read over your list. Look for patterns. Do most of your topics fall under one main category? If so, congratulations. It looks like you have a starting niche.

If not, don't worry. Spend a little more time thinking. See if any of the ideas on your paper spark other topic suggestions.

Think about the topics your family and friends ask you for advice about. Are you the go-to computer gal who provides better service than tech support? Do you know a lot about troubleshooting car problems? Are you a master organizer? Do you enjoy repurposing old items into something beautiful?

Use your skills and interests to help you pick a niche for your blog.

THREE COMMON FEARS ABOUT PICKING A NICHE

It's common to feel nervous about picking a niche. I often hear people say:

1. *I'm not an expert in any area.*
2. *What if I pick the wrong niche?*
3. *I have too many interests to pick just one.*

People tend to use these excuses as a reason for not blogging. The fear of picking the wrong niche stops their progress completely.

Don't let fear stop you from starting.

FEAR #1: I'M NOT AN EXPERT

Contrary to popular belief, you don't have to be an expert at a topic to successfully blog about it.

You know why? Because even though a fourth grader doesn't yet know everything, a fourth grader *is* an expert in the eyes of a second grader.

You have knowledge. You have skills. You know more than some people. Your unique insight is valuable.

So, your goal is to write to the people who can benefit from what you offer. There will always be people who know more than you, or who do more than you. Those people are not your ideal audience.

But there are others who need you. Write for them.

FEAR #2: WHAT IF I PICK THE WRONG NICHE?

Picking the wrong niche is a very real possibility. You may not pick the perfect one right from the start. But if you don't start somewhere, you'll never get the opportunity to learn from the experience. Picking the wrong niche brings you one step closer to finding the right one.

Here are some warning signs you picked the wrong niche:

1. Your posts aren't getting shares, likes, or comments.
2. You don't enjoy your topic.
3. You can't easily brainstorm blog post ideas.
4. You can't find any other bloggers making money in the niche you selected.

These signs all indicate that you may need to tweak your niche. Listen to your audience and your gut, then start tweaking. Many successful bloggers shifted their focus over time when they realized what they were doing wasn't working anymore.

Alee King started The Beautified Life as a beauty and lifestyle blog, but she realized she didn't want to write about this topic forever. Her true passion was in blogging and helping other moms create profitable blogs. She made the switch and her blog's stats and profits soared.

Your niche isn't set in stone. If you decide you picked the wrong one, shift your focus and pivot. You may lose some readers who decide they don't like the new direction you're taking, but that doesn't matter. Losing readers who are no longer in your target market is okay.

FEAR #3: I HAVE TOO MANY INTERESTS

Humans are beings with multiple passions. You have many interests and skills. The thought of picking just one feels limiting.

Don't worry that you're locking yourself in a tiny box by picking a niche. Your readers will want to get to know you. As you share your story and interests on the blog, you can offer insight into other aspects of your life, as well.

Perhaps you could add a "behind the scenes" post every Friday. Or publish a round-up post of items you love every other Tuesday. Don't be afraid to experiment. You can try something and see if your audience likes it or not.

Just make sure you aren't experimenting so often that no one remembers what the focus of your blog is.

In the introduction to this book, Sally shared how she struggled with having too many interests. Her solution was to find a common theme and write for one person. I talk more about how to identify your ideal reader later in this chapter.

CREATING YOUR IDEAL READER

Once you have a general idea of what you want to write about, it is time to figure out who your audience is. You need to create an ideal reader persona for your blog.

This step helps you get to know your readers. The more you learn about who is reading your blog, the more you can help them. And when you provide helpful content, you pull in readers who stick around and share your content with their friends and followers.

Before you make any more plans for your blog, or create a single piece of content, you need to nail down your ideal reader. Everything you do on your blog should speak to this reader.

> *Writing a blog post: Is it a topic your reader cares about?*
> *Building a product: Does it solve a problem your reader struggles with?*
> *Sharing a blurb on social media: Will the words and images resonate with your reader?*
> *Creating a graphic: Is the style one your reader enjoys?*
> *Recording a video: Does it speak to your reader?*

Every aspect of your blog must work together for a single purpose: to serve your reader.

WHO IS YOUR IDEAL READER?

The more information you have about your reader, the easier it is to monetize your blog. As you think about your ideal reader, consider their characteristics. Here are five aspects to think about:

1. Demographics
2. Personality
3. Social habits
4. Media habits
5. Money habits

In the following sections, I dive deeper into each of these five aspects. We've also created a free workbook that guides you through the steps to define your ideal reader and start your blog. You can download the workbook from the bonus area: sallyannmiller.com/bloggingbook

DEMOGRAPHICS OF YOUR IDEAL READER

Who is your ideal reader? Where do they live? What do they do? Demographics of your reader might include:

> Gender
> Age
> Location
> Level of education

> Income level

> Profession

PERSONALITY

The more you know about your ideal reader, the easier it is to craft content they will love. You need to dive deep into their personality. Here are some aspects of your reader's personality to consider:

> What are their interests?

> What do they do in their spare time?

> What prominent personality traits do they have?

> What are three adjectives used to describe this person?

> What are your reader's secret hopes and dreams?

> What would she most like to change about her life right now?

> What are her biggest problems or challenges?

> What keeps her awake at night?

> What kind of content would deliver exactly what she needs?

SOCIAL HABITS

Next, make sure you know where your ideal reader hangs out. Which of these networks does your reader use? How often are they on each?

> Pinterest

> Facebook

> Twitter

> Google+

> Snapchat

> YouTube

> Instagram

> LinkedIn

> Other

MEDIA HABITS

How will your ideal reader access your content?
> Which browser does your reader use?
> Do they favor a PC, tablet, or phone?
> Does your ideal reader prefer written, audio, or video content?

MONEY HABITS

Lastly, think about your reader's money habits. Here are some prompts to help you:
> What is your reader's relationship with money?
> What problems would they gladly pay for someone else to solve?
> What are your reader's favorite splurges?
> How does your reader primarily shop? (In the store? Online?)
> What stores does she frequent?

CREATING A PERSONA TAKES TIME

Answering all these questions about your ideal reader won't happen overnight. You may need to do some research, especially to learn more about social media use.

To research your audience, go where you think your target market is and start gathering data. Look at common questions on online forums like Quora. Check out questions in Facebook Groups or on other social media platforms. Read reviews of books you think your audience is reading on Amazon. See what information is missing, and what types of content they love.

If your friends are your idea reader, talk to them. Spend some time chatting about hopes, dreams, challenges, and habits. Listen and learn.

As you gather more information, use it to write down everything you can about your reader. The more details you capture, the better.

Naming your reader helps make them more personable. Then write a paragraph or two describing this person.

Here's an example:

Andrea is a thirty-two year old stay-at-home mom to her four young children. While she enjoys being home, she misses the career she had before having kids. She knows the budget could use a little boost and wishes there was some way she could earn money from home-- without getting scammed.

But between dishes and laundry and the kids needing her, she doesn't believe she has time to work. There's just no margin in her life, and she's constantly overwhelmed. Social media is a fun outlet, and she enjoys interacting with friends and family on Facebook. She spends quite a bit of time looking for ways to streamline life on Pinterest. She knows if she could just figure out this time thing, she would be unstoppable.

When you first create this persona, you may make some assumptions. And you may make them incorrectly.

It's okay if this isn't perfect. Your ideal reader may change over time.

You can always add more details and make changes as you go. Just don't spend a ton of time creating content when you don't know who it's for.

Your ideal readers are out there. You just have to find them.

ACTION STEPS

Throughout this book, I ask you to complete action steps. Please don't skip the action steps. If you don't act, you won't see results. Having said that, don't stress about racing to the finish line. This is your journey. So, take things at your own pace.

Starting a blog can be overwhelming. There's a lot to learn and do. To help you break the process into more manageable steps, we've created a free workbook for you. The workbook covers the action steps you will find in this book and includes additional prompts to help you keep moving forward and tackle each step at the right time.

Download the workbook from the bonus area: sallyannmiller.com/bloggingbook

1. Answer the questions at the start of this chapter and pick a niche for your blog.

2. Follow the directions in this chapter to create a persona for your blog's ideal reader.

You now have a clear picture of who you're writing for and what you're going to write about. You're ready to share your passion with the world. In the next chapter, I teach you how to set up your blog so you can get started right away.

CHAPTER TWO

Set Up Your Blog

Now that you know who you're writing for, and you're ready to make money blogging, it's time to set up your blog. But first, there's something important you need to know about this process.

IT COSTS MONEY TO START AN INCOME-GENERATING BLOG

But don't worry, starting a blog doesn't cost a fortune. I'm going to show you exactly how to set up your blog for less than $100.

Technically, you can start a blog without spending any money. Sites like Blogger and WordPress.com make it possible.

But if you plan to build an income-generating blog, don't start there. You see, on those free sites, you don't own your blog. It's like renting a house instead of buying it.

When you rent, there are rules and regulations about what you can and can't do. You might be able to hang up a picture (with removable putty), but you can't repaint the walls on a whim. You don't have total control of the property, because it belongs to someone else.

Like landlords, free blogging platforms have preexisting conditions you must abide by. You have to follow all the rules in the Terms of Service for your blog platform. For instance, there are strict rules concerning advertisements and sponsored content. If you violate these conditions, you risk losing your blog. And you don't want to deal with a blogging eviction.

Control isn't the only thing you gain by shelling out the money for a self-hosted blog. You also have more options. When you create your blog on a free platform, you can't install many popular plugins, themes, or widgets.

These features help improve your readers' experience, and they allow you to choose your blog's layout and theme. Now, if all of this sounds like a foreign language, don't worry. In the rest of this chapter, I explain each of these terms and exactly how to set up your blog.

There's one more reason why you will want to build a self-hosted blog. It gives you credibility. When you give out your domain name, it looks like this:

yourdomainname.com

If you run on a free platform, your domain looks like this:

yourdomainname.blogspot.com or *yourdomainname.wordpress.com*

See the difference? Which domain are you going to remember more easily? Which one looks more professional?

Owning your own blog and domain sets you up as a pro. It shows that you believe in yourself enough to invest in you. And if you don't believe in you, why should anyone else?

The exact amount of money you need to start a blog depends on your goals. I recommend starting small, spending the least amount possible at first. Then, as you begin making money, reinvest your profits back into your blog.

Once you find your niche and audience, you can ramp things up. Invest in professional design, technical support, and marketing help. In this chapter, I show you how to start a blog for less than $100. Here are the steps to create your blog:

1. Buy a domain. This is your blog's address. For example: mynewblog.com.

2. Buy hosting. This is where the files related to your blog are stored.

3. Select a content management system. I recommend WordPress.

4. Select a free or paid theme. This determines your blog's look and style.

5. Install plugins and widgets to customize your blog.

6. Create blog content in the form of website pages and posts.

Ready to get started? Let's dive in and create your blog. The first step is to pick a website name and buy a domain.

BUYING A DOMAIN

Your domain is your blog's address. When visitors head to your blog, they enter your domain in the address bar.

A domain typically costs between $10 and $20 per year, though you may be able to snag one for much less if you pick it up during a sale. You can also save if you pick up a multi-year renewal instead of a single year.

You can buy your domain through your host or buy it from a different company. Most of my domains are from GoDaddy.com because they offer a good price. Feel free to shop around and see what you can find.

DOMAIN AVAILABILITY

You may not be able to get the domain name of your dreams. Someone else may already own it. And when someone else owns the domain you want, it costs a lot more to get it. Sometimes thousands of dollars more.

When I launched my second site, I really wanted to use my first and last name. Branding myself was the goal. However, my name as a domain was already taken, so I had to think a bit.

Since I was launching a freelance writing site, I decided to throw "writing" at the end. It worked, and I got my domain lisatannerwriting.com. It's not exactly what I wanted, but it was available and the price was right.

Don't stress too much about your domain name. Pick one you like that makes the most sense. You can successfully market almost any name.

But if you spend all your time thinking and overanalyzing, you will never take action. Action is what brings in the money.

HOW TO NAME YOUR BLOG

If you don't already have a name in mind, here are eight tips for finding the perfect name for your blog.

1. Consider branding yourself. This is where you use your name as the domain (or a variation of it if your name is already taken like mine was).

2. Spend some time brainstorming words related to your niche. Write down everything that comes to mind.

3. Look over your ideas and see which ones stand out to you the most.

4. Try a variety of combinations and say each one out loud.

5. Make sure your words are straightforward to spell and not easily confused. For example, "for," "four," and "4" can all be in a domain. Using words with multiple meanings can confuse potential readers who are trying to find you.

6. Shorter is better. People have short attention spans these days. Don't make them remember a long phrase.

7. Stick to a .com domain if possible. It's the default most people remember, and changing it up might look cool, but it may cause confusion.

8. Pick something other people won't mind sharing. Your audience can be your guide, but don't use controversial words or words that can be interpreted as disparaging in your domain.

HOSTING

Once you have a domain, you need a hosting company. Web hosts make it possible for visitors to see your website. They store all the files related to your website (coding, text, images, etc.) on their servers. When a visitor goes to your website, the server will deliver the information to them so they can view the site.

Without a host, you can't publish your website. There are tons of web hosts available. Most offer the services a beginning blogger needs.

My first self-hosted website was hosted by GoDaddy, though I eventually moved it over to BlueHost, so I only had to pay for one multi-site plan.

I stayed with BlueHost for a couple years, but I no longer recommend it for new or experienced bloggers. I recently moved over to FastComet, because my blogs were experiencing more hosting errors which resulted in downtime.

At first the downtime was just an annoyance. I would log in to add a post, and I'd get an error. After a few minutes, I was able to log in and work.

But the errors started occurring more frequently and lasting longer. As a busy mom, I don't always have a lot of time to work. Not being able to access my blog when I had time was frustrating.

I also heard from two readers about my sites being down. I knew I had to do something to keep my websites up and running more consistently. I contacted the person I hire for blog maintenance, and he recommended I switch to FastComet.

Since switching, I haven't had a single error message or any trouble logging in. Plus, my site loads more quickly. FastComet has more servers and data centers than BlueHost.

After my move was complete, I requested and received a prorated refund from BlueHost. Because I purchased during an end-of-the-year sale, I actually paid less for FastComet than I did for BlueHost.

No matter which host you go with, here are five key things to look for:

1. Customer support (when your blog goes down, you will want help.)
2. Reliability (so your blog is up when people want to visit.)
3. Reputation (the host will have access to all your personal information and all your blog files.)
4. Security (you don't want to be hacked.)
5. Fixed pricing (you don't want any unexpected surprises partway through the year.)

START SMALL

You don't need all the bells and whistles to get a blog started. Pick a plan with the basics. You can always upgrade later. To get your first blog up and running, the single website plan is a good place to start. It's typically the lowest tier of pricing.

Depending on your host and the tier you select, you can expect to spend between $2.95 to $14.99 per month to host your blog.

> *Tip: When I first paid for hosting, I was planning to pay for a month of service and thought it'd be around $3. However, I learned you pay for at least a year of hosting at once. Make sure you multiply your monthly commitment by 12 to learn how much you'll need to pay upfront.*

Now that I've switched hosts, I discovered FastComet does offer a monthly payment plan. If money is really tight, this might be a good solution!

A NOTE ABOUT YOUR PRIVACY

Legally, you must give your name, address, and phone number when you register a website. This information is then available for people to see.

If you don't like the idea of sharing your real address with the world, you have two options.

1. Pay for a privacy service through your web host.

2. Pay for a PO box.

If someone tries to look up who owns a website without a domain privacy service, they can see your contact information, including your address. If you have the domain privacy service in place, all they see is the contact information for the privacy company. This service helps protect your information.

Depending on your location, a PO box may cost more than a year of privacy service. But since you'll also need to include your address in any emails you send to your email list (more on that in chapter four), I think this option is a better choice in the long run.

Of course, you can do both. Many bloggers pay for the privacy service and a PO box. Let your budget and your concern for privacy guide your decision. You can find out how much a PO box in your area costs on the USPS website.

TOTAL COSTS FOR YOUR BLOG'S FIRST YEAR

How much does it cost to start a blog? Here's a breakdown of the costs for your first year:

Domain: $10

Basic Hosting: $35.88 (assuming a $2.99/month plan)

PO Box: $45 (give or take a little based on location)

Total: $90.88

For less than $100 you can have everything you need to get your blog up and running for a year. You may have other costs. For example, if you select a paid theme instead of a free one, you will be paying more. But these are optional.

CONTENT MANAGEMENT SYSTEM: WORDPRESS

Now that you have a domain and a host, you need a content management system for your blog. This allows you to customize your site and add content.

There are a couple of content management systems available, but I recommend WordPress.org. Make sure you use WordPress.org, which is the self-hosted version, and not WordPress.com, which is hosted by WrodPress and has some limitations.

It's what many bloggers use, and it's popular for a reason. Since many bloggers use it, there are thousands of themes available. You can easily find technical support. It's also very customizable and flexible. You can make your site look exactly like you want it to.

Many hosting companies install WordPress for you for free. Be sure to ask if yours does, too. Once you have WordPress installed, it's time to log in to your account and get some prep work done.

SELECT A THEME

Your theme contains several files detailing important information about the design of your website. It holds the coding for the:
> Style of your website
> Colors of your website
> Layout of different pages
> Location of your menus
> Widget display areas
> Styles for posts and pages

A theme dictates the styling details for your site. By changing the theme, you change how it looks.

A professional-looking theme makes your site more visually attractive. You want your site to look nice, or your visitors won't stay around to read your content.

The good news? You can start with a free theme. Just be careful which one you select, because there are some terrible free themes out there! There are three important things to look for when selecting a theme:
1. Mobile responsive design
2. Compatibility
3. Documentation and support

On her blog, Sally provides a step-by-step guide to set up your blog with a free theme that looks professional and meets the above criteria. You can find the article at: sallyannmiller.com/how-to-start-a-successful-blog/

MOBILE-RESPONSIVE DESIGN

According to comScore, 69 percent of user media time is spent on smartphones. Your website must accommodate your mobile users.

Your theme needs to utilize a mobile-responsive design. It should shift so it is easy to read on any screen size. You can use Google's Mobile Friendly Test to find out how mobile-friendly a site is.

COMPATIBILITY

There are many browsers available for Internet users (Firefox, Internet Explorer, Chrome, and more). Since you don't know which ones your visitors will be using, you need a theme that will be compatible with a variety of web browsers.

You can test this yourself once you install a theme. Just open up your site on several different browsers, including on your smartphone.

Make sure your site looks good and click a couple of links to ensure everything works properly.

DOCUMENTATION AND SUPPORT

The instruction manual for a theme is known as its documentation. Make sure some is available for whatever theme you select.

You will also want to know exactly what support is available. Some developers of free themes don't offer any support, which means you may need to hire someone if a problem arises. Other developers offer support through forums, live chat, or email.

The documentation and support details should be listed. Understand what you're getting before you spend too much time customizing the theme.

INSTALL AND CUSTOMIZE YOUR THEME

Once you select a theme, you need to install it. To do that, log into your WordPress site. Then, over on the left-hand side, you'll see the word Appearance. Click on that, and then navigate to Themes.

If your theme is one that's already on WordPress, type the name of it into the search bar. When you find it, click on it and select "Install." If you've purchased your theme, follow the directions you were given to download your theme as a .zip file. Then click on the Upload Theme button to install it.

When your theme is installed, you will have the option to preview and activate. Before any visitors see your new theme, you need to activate it.

After activation, your theme is ready for customization. Since each theme is different, you need to rely on the documentation to make changes. For most themes, you need to customize the:

1. Blog name and tagline
2. Logo or header image
3. Default blog colors
4. Font for headings and regular paragraphs (this is only necessary if you don't like the default font used by your theme.)

These basic steps will get your site ready for publishing. You can continue making changes after it's live.

If you're struggling with the technical steps, check out this article on Sally's blog: sallyannmiller.com/how-to-start-a-successful-blog/. It shows the exact steps to create your blog using FastComet hosting and a free WordPress theme.

PLUGINS

Whew! There's a lot ground to cover when you're getting a money-making blog set up.

If you're feeling overwhelmed, don't worry. This is normal. Take a deep breath and tackle one step at a time. You've got this.

Once your WordPress theme is installed, you need to add a few plugins to help you on your blogging journey.

A plugin adds functions or features to your site. There are tons of plugins available, but don't spend time researching them all right now. As you learn more about blogging and gain some experience, you can add additional plugins to your site.

There are some plugins you will need to install upfront. These help you get your blog started on the right foot. Here's a peek at ten plugins I use and recommend, with a brief explanation of each one. As a bare minimum, I recommend using YoastSEO, Askimet Anti-Spam, and Jetpack.

1. YoastSEO

We talk more about SEO (search engine optimization) later, but basically it helps Google find your website. It's important! This plugin ensures each blog post is ready for publication from an SEO perspective.

2. Askimet Anti-Spam

You don't want a bunch of spam comments taking over your blog. Help keep them at bay with this plugin. How do you recognize spam comments? Well, they:

> Are vague (e.g. "great post")
> Contain more than one URL
> Contain several misspellings
> Don't make any sense
> Aren't related to your topic
> Ask you to search for something

Sometimes spam comments are easy to recognize. Here's one Askimet caught for me recently:

> *"I see you don't monetize your website, don't waste your traffic, you can earn extra bucks every month because you've got high quality content. If you want to know how to make extra bucks, search for: Mertiso's tips best adsense alternative"*

This comment has plenty of red flags. First, it makes an incorrect assumption about my site. I do monetize. Second, it asks me to search for a specific keyword phrase. It is definitely spam.

But spam isn't always obvious. Sometimes it looks something like this:

> *"I was suggested this blog by my cousin. You are wonderful. I will be back."*

At first glance, it appears to be a compliment. However, this comment adds nothing of value to the conversation. It is generic and could be left on any blog post. It is spam.

3. CommentLuv

It's important to build a sense of community on your blog. Comments are one way to do that. This plugin allows commenters to link to their latest blog post.

4. Pinterest PinIt Button

You can drive a lot of traffic to your blog from Pinterest. Make it easy for your visitors to pin your content with a PinIt button on each image.

5. Google Analytics for WordPress

You can't make the right decisions for your blog without analyzing some data. Google Analytics is a reliable source of information. Get it connected to your site from the start. The numbers it provides show you what's working, and what's not.

6. Molongui Authorship

You want an author bio after each post so everyone can learn more about you. With this plugin, you can decide to show or hide the bio on each post. You can also add multiple authors. If you have guest posts, you can credit the writer and link back to their site.

7. Jetpack

The Jetpack plugin adds many features to your site. Here are five important ones:
> Track basic stats
> Show social sharing icons underneath your content
> Compress images
> Create a sitemap
> Create basic contact forms

You need to create a free WordPress.com account to use this plugin.

8. Broken Link Checker

Links go down. But it takes time to constantly go back through all your old content and make sure you aren't leading your readers to a website page that no longer exists. Link checker to the rescue. It keeps checking your site and notifies you when it finds a problem. Then you can fix it.

9. No Self Pings

Have you ever noticed pingbacks in the comments section of a blog? Those occur when your post gets linked to. When blogging, you want to link to your old content, but you don't want all those pingbacks showing. This plugin prevents that from happening.

10. WP Super Cache

A fast website makes visitors happy. This plugin helps make your site load faster. There are plenty of caching plugins out there, but this one is free, user-friendly, and reliable.

WIDGETS

Widgets refer to small blocks on your website that each perform one task. You can easily add these to your sidebars, headers, and footers to help customize the function and appearance of your site.

There are too many widgets available to cover them all, especially since different themes have different widgets available. But here are five common ones you can install on your blog.

1. Email Marketing

With a widget, you can let your readers sign up for your newsletter from a simple form in your sidebar.

2. Images

Image widgets allow you to embed an image and link it to a URL. When readers click on the image, they go to the site linked.

3. Social Media

A variety of social media widgets exist. Two common types allow readers to follow you on a specific platform or show your feeds.

4. Search Bar

Give your readers the option of easily searching through your archives with a search bar widget.

5. Popular Posts

To encourage readers to check out your popular content, install a popular posts widget. It provides an image and a link to your top posts.

While you are customizing your website, take some time to explore the widgets available to you.

PAGES VS. POSTS

From your WordPress dashboard, you can create pages and posts. Your posts are what you publish on your blog. We cover these in detail in chapter five.

Pages are different. They aren't typically updated as often, and they provide information for your readers. When you set up your blog, you want to create at least three pages: a home page, an about page, and a contact page. Below is an overview of each of these. More details are provided in chapter four.

Your home page is what readers see when they type in your URL. You can decide if you want a static home page, or if you want your blog to be your home page.

I used my blog as my home page for years, but recently switched to a static one. This means my home page is always the same, even though my blog posts are changing. On this page, I provide some information for my readers to share the purpose of my blog and provide links to popular posts.

Decide which route you want to go with. You can change it later, though, so don't get stuck here.

Your about page tells people a bit more about you and your blog. But it's not all about you. Make sure you share how your reader will benefit from your knowledge and content.

Finally, your contact page allows readers to get in touch with you. It typically includes an online form they can fill out. You can configure this to go to your email so you will be notified. Some bloggers also include an email address on this page.

WHEN TO HIT PUBLISH

Until you hit Publish, your blog won't be live. Visitors who type in your URL will see a "Coming Soon" page or something similar.

Here are a few things you will need to do before you hit the button. The first two tasks were covered in this chapter. The rest is covered in more detail later.

1. Set up your theme.
2. Spend a little time customizing it.
3. Create a contact page (so your readers can get in touch).
4. Create an about page (so your readers know who you are and what your blog is about).
5. Post three blog posts with images for sharing.

When you're ready, it's time to go live! But first, let's talk about the reason why most aspiring bloggers never get started, as I don't want this to happen to you.

DON'T LET PERFECTION STOP YOU

Starting a blog can be overwhelming. There are *so many* options available. You have to make *so many* decisions. And getting the blog published is a stumbling block for many would-be bloggers. They freeze, unable to move forward until they think it's perfect. Here's what helped me overcome this feeling:

I finally realized perfect wasn't going to happen. After this realization, I had two choices.

1. Continue learning, making changes, researching, and tweaking until I gained enough confidence to hit publish. Which would likely *never* happen.

2. Hit publish now and tweak as I go.

I picked option two. And you know what? My blog was *ugly* in the early stages! I didn't know what I was doing. I picked fonts that didn't pair well. My colors were a bit much. I changed themes at least five times my first year. My blog got many facelifts as I learned new tricks.

And eventually I paid and got a nice theme installed. I paid for a logo from a professional designer. My site looks 100 times better than it did when I started.

But you know what? It still isn't perfect. It never will be. And neither will yours. There's no such thing as a perfect blog design. If there was, everyone would be using it. Then it wouldn't be perfect anymore because it'd be overused.

Don't let the quest for perfection stop you from starting a blog. Get something out that's not perfect, then make changes as you learn more and gain confidence with your skills (or make money and can pay someone else).

ACTION STEPS

1. Brainstorm a blog name and research the availability of the URL.

2. Research web host companies and see who has the best deal. (FastComet is a good starting place).

3. Purchase a year of hosting and a domain.

4. Select, install, and activate a theme.

5. Customize your site with plugins and widgets.

Now that your blog is set up, you're ready to plan your content. In the next chapter, I will show you how to create a content calendar, so you'll always know what you need to write about.

CHAPTER THREE

Plan Your Content

N ow that you have the backbone of your blog in place, it's time to plan your content. Remember, without a plan, you won't have a money-making blog. I can't stress the importance of content planning enough. To help you implement the steps in this chapter, I've created an additional resource. It's a step-by-step guide on how to create your content calendar. You can download the worksheet from the bonus area: sallyannmiller.com/bloggingbook

CONSISTENCY MATTERS

How often do you plan to post new content to your blog? No matter what you choose as the perfect posting schedule for you and your readers, you must be consistent.

It's better to post twice a month, every month, than to post three times a week one month and then nothing for a couple of months.

The more consistent you are, the more likely it is that your readers will return. So, pick a schedule that's realistic. If life is crazy, and you're busy taking care of the kids and running the house, you won't have time to post every single day.

Don't set yourself up for failure.

What number comes to mind when you first think about your posting frequency? Now, cut it in half. Then, stick to that number. At least at first. If you have extra time, you can write posts in advance and schedule them. We'll discuss this in the upcoming chapters.

You can always increase your posting schedule later if you want.

CREATE CATEGORIES

Can you break your niche down into a couple of topics? This is how you think of categories for your blog. For instance, on my site, I write about:

> Working from home with kids
> Building a freelance business
> Growing a blog as a busy mom
> Time management

Those topics are the main categories on my blog. When I'm brainstorming content, I try to get at least a couple of post ideas from each category. This helps me keep my blog well rounded, without becoming super heavy in any one area.

Try to think of three or four categories you can cover on your blog. Make sure they all make sense and fall within your niche. And keep it simple. You should use categories your readers easily understand instead of cute names.

BRAINSTORMING POST TOPICS

Once your categories are written down, you can start brainstorming. This is one of my favorite parts of the blogging process because it's so creative.

Get out a piece of paper and set a timer for ten minutes. Write down anything you can think of related to each of your categories, and your niche in general.

Don't evaluate ideas right now, just write them all down. Your goal is to come up with as many ideas as possible. Once your time is up, read all the ideas aloud. This step helps you better evaluate what you have.

Look for patterns. Are there any ideas that you could turn into a series? Could you combine some ideas into a longer post? Will any of the suggestions not work? Go ahead and cross them out. Which four or five ideas sound most interesting to you? Circle those.

On another piece of paper, write down the ideas you circled. Then, write down any of your other ideas that you think will be a good fit for your blog. You now have your first twenty or more post ideas.

SEO BASICS

Before you get too far into your content planning, you need to know a little about SEO (Search Engine Optimization) and keywords. An SEO strategy helps you connect with the people who need what you have to offer. It gets the right traffic to your site.

Keywords play an important part in SEO. Keywords help people find your blog. They tell Google (and other search engines) what your post is about. Keywords are simply what people type into search engines while looking for information. They can be short:

> Dogs

> Blogging tips

> Pumpkin recipes

Or long:

> How do you housetrain a puppy?

> Blogging tips for beginning bloggers

> Gluten-free pumpkin recipes

The longer keyword phrases are more specific. These are long-tail keywords. As a beginning blogger, you should focus on long-tail keywords. There are many blogs out there. And with all the information available, you will want to deliver exactly what people are looking for.

Your blog may get buried on page 1,036 when someone searches for just a short keyword. People frankly aren't going to see it on the search results. But, if you optimize a post with a long-tail keyword, your post is much more likely to come up on top.

For instance, here are three long-tail keywords that have brought me to the first page of Google:

> Freelancing with kids

> Freelancing with a baby

> Family writing time

These are all topics I cover extensively on my blog. Because I have used a long-tail keyword strategy with SEO, Google is helping those who want to learn more about these topics find my blog.

KEYWORD RESEARCH WITH PINTEREST

Finding keywords used to feel like a mystery to me. I didn't want to pay for access to keyword researchers. And I didn't think I had time to spend researching keywords, anyway.

But I was wrong. I discovered a streamlined, free way to research keywords for my blog. I learned to find keywords using Pinterest.

Pinterest is not just another social media platform. It is a search engine, like Google. It's just a visual one.

When someone searches for a topic on Pinterest, they are using keywords. They're asking the search engine to send back information related to that topic. Then Pinterest scours its data. It looks for the keywords in the pin descriptions and titles. When it gets a hit, it sends it back to the user in the results.

Since it works like Google, you can use Pinterest to research keywords for your blog posts. To do this, you need to use Pinterest's search bar.

When you start, make sure you have your list of blog post ideas from earlier in this chapter on hand. Pick a topic and type it into the search bar on Pinterest. As you type, Pinterest suggests keyword phrases based on what you enter. These are all potential long-tail keywords you can plan your post around. Let's look at an example.

If you want to write about time management, type "time management" into Pinterest's search bar. These potential keywords might appear:

> Time management tips

> Time management for moms

> Time management printables

> Time management quotes

Do any of those long-tail keywords identify what you want to write about? If so, pick one and use that to form the SEO backbone of your post. This simply means that you incorporate the keyword into your blog post. At a minimum, you want to include the keyword in your post title, the opening paragraph, and at least one section header. I talk more about how to use keywords for SEO later in this chapter.

If you need to, try searching again with slightly different words. You want to use words that your ideal reader from chapter one would search for.

Once you have your long-tail keyword for this topic, pick another one. Keep going until you have keywords selected for each of your post ideas.

KEYWORD RESEARCH WITH KWFINDER

What happens if your audience isn't on Pinterest? You can use another tool to research keywords. Sally uses and recommends KWFinder.

You can type a search term into KWFinder and it displays data for that term. It also suggests other related keywords. One useful feature is the difficulty score. This tells you whether it's easy or difficult to appear on Google's first page for the search term. Of course, you need to target "easy" keywords.

When you sign up for a free account with KWFinder, you can do five keyword searches per day. If you do this every day for a week you can find the keywords that work best for your readers.

FIND YOUR ANGLE

A list of keywords is nice, but it's not everything you need to craft a great blog post. You must look at each keyword and decide which angle you will use to cover the topic.

There are several angles for every topic. Some topics work well as a how-to guide. Others are more of a step-by-step tutorial, or a roundup of several ideas. For example, if you want to write a blog post about time management tips, here are six angles you could try:

1. Write a round-up of ten different time management tips your audience can use.

2. Write an in-depth tutorial of each tip.

3. Provide a review of tools you use to help with time management.

4. Compare and contrast two different time management tools.

5. Write a case study showing how you gained a certain amount of time by implementing three different time management tips.

6. Write about what your readers can do with their newfound time.

Read over your blog post ideas again. Write down an angle to use for each one. Remember you can always change it later if it turns out to be a bad fit. Each post you write should meet your reader's needs. Ask yourself why your readers want to read the post you are planning.

I will dive deeper into content creation in chapter five.

WRITE YOUR HEADLINE

Once you have the keyword and angle for your posts, you can write your headline. Headlines are important. People see your headline and make a judgment call. Are they intrigued enough to click through, or should they keep scrolling and skip it?

| *Your headline must be good, or you'll lose your readers.*

It took me a long time to learn about the importance of headlines. I used to create cute headlines for my posts, throwing in an extra dash of alliteration just because I could.

As I look back through some of my early blog posts, I cringe at the headlines I used. No wonder no one was reading my blog. They had no incentive to click through.

THE ANATOMY OF A GOOD HEADLINE

What makes a good headline? Your headline must do these seven things:

1. Intrigue the reader.
2. Explain what the reader will learn.
3. Be between 8 to 14 words.
4. Be around 70 characters in length including space (so the headline will show in its entirety on Google and other search engines).
5. The headline should not lie to or mislead readers about the actual content of the post (stay away from clickbait).
6. Provide a clue to the type of post it'll be.
7. Encourage sharing.

Even though my headline-writing skills have improved since my alliteration days, I'm still not a pro at writing great headlines. Thankfully, there's a tool to help. You can sign up for a free account with Headline Analyzer from CoSchedule and enter a draft of your headline. Then, it scores your headline for you. A score of 70 or higher is a headline worth keeping. Any lower than that, and you should keep tweaking.

If you scroll down after entering your headline, you will find plenty of suggestions to help you improve. Keep trying new combinations of words, or different phrases.

Here's a peek at six titles I tried for a recent blog post, with the score each received. The final idea is the one I went with.

1. How to Find Great Blog Post Ideas (67)
2. 10 Different Ways to Find Blog Post Ideas (60)
3. 10 Quick Strategies to Brainstorm Blog Post Ideas (62)
4. How to Quickly Find Blog Post Ideas as a Busy Mom (68)
5. How to Easily Find Great Blog Post Ideas (70)
6. How to Quickly Find Great Blog Post Ideas (72)

It took me a while to come up with a winning headline. However, it's worth the effort. Good headlines get more shares and page views.

Take some time and use the Headline Analyzer to create working headlines for each of your blog post ideas. This step helps you create your posts more quickly.

TEN HEADLINE FORMULAS

To give you a head start planning your headline, here are ten fill-in-the-blank formulas that are proven to work. See if you can tweak any of these to work for what you want to write about.

Notice there is one key ingredient in each of these headlines. They each need to focus on something your reader cares about. Because if they don't, it doesn't matter what your headline says; your readers won't be interested.

1. How to [do something your reader cares about]
2. [Number] Hacks to [something your reader cares about]
3. [Number] Reasons You're Not [outcome readers care about]
4. The Number One Trick to [achieving an outcome your readers care about]
5. Little Known Ways to [do something your readers care about]
6. [Ask a question to peek the curiosity of your reader]
7. How I [achieved something specific your reader cares about] in [period of time]
8. The [strong adjective] Guide to [something your reader cares about]
9. Why I Don't [something others in your niche do, and probably some of your readers]
10. [Number] [strong adjective] Things You Need to [something your reader cares about]

Are these the only headlines you can use? Of course not! But they're a good starting point. The more you write, the more you will discover what appeals to your readers.

PLAN YOUR CONTENT CALENDAR

If you are following along, you now have several headlines for future posts. Now it's time to put these on your content calendar.

A content calendar helps you keep track of the posts you plan to publish on your blog. It's an important tool to help you stay organized.

Having a plan for your content improves your blogging consistency and quality. When you don't have to spend time thinking about what to write, you have more energy to put into the actual writing.

Content calendars also allow you to plan more strategically. You can prepare for upcoming holidays and events and take advantage of important keywords during those times.

How far in advance you plan your content is up to you. I typically prepare a month-long content calendar, though I have tried a quarter-long one. Experiment and see what works for you.

A content calendar doesn't need to be fancy. You can use an actual calendar, a piece of paper, an app, or a plug-in for your WordPress site. What it looks like isn't important. Finding a method that works for you is.

There's no point in creating a fancy content calendar if you won't use it. Here's how to get started planning your content calendar:

1. Decide when you want to publish blog posts in the next month. Then, write down each date in your content calendar.

2. Next, look at your headlines. Read them aloud so they are fresh in your mind. Are any of them seasonal? Do any relate to upcoming holidays? Do any posts go together in a series? Which one needs to be published first?

3. Use your best judgment and assign one headline to each of the dates you plan to publish.

Fantastic! You've now planned your blog content for the next month (or longer). It's time to write your first blog post.

YOUR FIRST BLOG POST

Many would-be bloggers get stuck on their first post. Here's my advice to you:

> *Just write something and hit publish. I promise it gets easier the more you do it.*

Your first post should be written with your ideal reader in mind. Most bloggers stick with one of these two methods for the first post:

1. Write an introduction post letting your readers know what to expect.
2. Jump into your regular content and pick one to be first.

Either is fine. Just choose one and go. Don't spend too much time thinking about it. On one of my blogs, I started with an introduction post. On the other, I jumped into regular content, but weaved a little bit of an introduction into it.

In chapter five, I will talk about how to write a compelling blog post. For now, focus on writing something. Anything. You can always go back and change or delete a post if you decide it doesn't work for you, but you can't get back the time you wasted trying to decide what to post.

ACTION STEPS

1. Follow the directions in this chapter to create a content calendar for the first month of your blog. To help you do this, you can download a step-by-step guide to creating a content calendar from the bonus area: sallyannmiller.com/bloggingbook

2. Pick the style you want to use for your first post.

Now you know what you're going to write about for the next month. Great work! In the next chapter, I will show you how to get your blog ready for readers. There's a little bit of prep work you will need to do before you start sharing your blog with the world.

CHAPTER FOUR

Get Ready for Readers

Before you have company over to your home, what do you do? Most people clean up the house a bit and make sure clean towels are hanging in the guest bathroom. You might take a few minutes to plan the food you'll serve. Taking time to prepare your house for guests helps them feel welcome. It's one way of showing that you care. Likewise, getting your blog ready for readers welcomes them and encourages them to stick around.

Let's look at seven steps you will need to take before you start inviting people to your blog through marketing.

AN ABOUT PAGE

This page tells readers who you are and what your blog is about. But don't make the mistake of thinking that the about page is all about you. It's not.

Your about page is your chance to show your ideal reader why your blog is a great fit for them. It's an opportunity to share how you can meet the needs of your target audience. This means you should share who you blog for. Tell potential visitors who your readers are. This will help them decide if they're in the right spot or not.

You should also:

> Share a couple of fun facts about yourself to make it personable.

> Include your name and a picture of you.

> Link to a couple of your most popular posts to encourage readers to check out some more of your work.

> Be honest and be yourself.

> Include a call to action (CTA) at the end. What should your reader do next? We'll cover CTAs in more detail later.

You can write your about page in first or third person (using "I" or your name). Either is acceptable. Just make sure you pick one and stick to it. Don't jump back and forth between the two.

Once you have your about page drafted, read it aloud. Does it sound like something you would say, or does it sound boring and dry?

Rework it a bit until you can read it easily and hear yourself actually saying the words on the page. Then ask a friend to read it for you. Can they think of anything you should add or take out?

CONTACT PAGE

You need a way for your readers to get in touch with you. A contact page is an easy solution.

If you have the Jetpack plugin installed, you can use it to create a basic contact page. Otherwise, you can install a contact form plugin such as Contact Form 7. Make sure you configure the plugin to send responses to your primary email address, then test it.

If desired, you can also list an email address for readers to use directly. Sometimes this can lead to unsolicited spam, though.

LEGAL REQUIREMENTS

While blogging is a fun and creative outlet, it's bound by certain laws. You must have certain information available on your blog for your readers.

Reminder: Laws change over time and are based on location. This chapter is for your information and is not legal advice. If you have questions, always seek advice from a qualified professional.

In the following sections, I cover four legal aspects of your blog:

1. SSL
2. Privacy Policy
3. Disclosure
4. Copyrights

SSL

In fall of 2017, Google started awarding small boosts in ranking to sites using SSL. SSL encrypts data and helps keep your users' information secure. Sites with SSL use an HTTPS: at the start of the url instead of HTTP:.

If you are selling products on your site and collecting payments directly (not through PayPal or Stripe), you need to have the encryption. It's your due diligence to protect your customers.

Most hosting companies provide free SSL certificates. I recommend checking with your hosting company to find out. If you can get one, it's worth using it. It is easy to figure out with FastComet, and there are plenty of video tutorials on YouTube to help you with this step.

PRIVACY POLICY

Do you collect any information from your readers? If you plan on setting up an email list, you will. If you use social share buttons, those can track user information as well.

It's important to have a privacy policy on your site, explaining what you do with the information you collect. For instance, your readers want to be confident you aren't going to sell their information to spammers.

You can find free privacy policy generators online. I opted to go with a paid policy from Iubenda. The $27 annual price tag was worth the peace of mind it brought, knowing it covered everything and was backed by lawyers.

Since I sell products on my site (my course and ebooks), I wanted the extra layer of protection. If you aren't doing that, a basic, free privacy policy will get you started just fine.

DISCLOSURE

You are required to disclose certain information to your readers. If you are compensated in any way (through money, free product, or another arrangement) for a post, you need to disclose that.

If you are using affiliate links and you receive a commission when your readers purchase through your link, you need to disclose that. Affiliate links are when you partner with another company or brand and promote their products to your audience. You earn a commission for any sales coming from your links. I cover how to make money as an affiliate in chapter eight.

There are very specific rules for disclosure. Here's a hint: If you are wondering if you should disclose, you probably should.

If you read blogs, you may know what a simple disclosure statement looks like. It typically says, "This post may contain affiliate links. If you click through and make a purchase, I will receive a small commission at no additional cost to you."

Where you place your disclosure matters from a legal standpoint. You must have the disclosure before the links. Your readers should not have to scroll all the way to the bottom of a post or page to discover this information. That's why many bloggers have a disclosure statement at the top of each post.

You also must meet disclosure guidelines for the companies you are an affiliate for. For instance, Amazon has a very specific blurb that must be on your website. Instead of putting this on every post that uses Amazon affiliate links, I have this information on a separate disclosure page.

That page specifies additional information about the companies I partner with. It spells out clearly that I may receive income from purchases made through my links.

THE LAW AND COPYRIGHTS

There's one more area of legal topics you need to know about as a blogger. Copyrights.

You do not have the right to share anything you'd like on your blog. If someone else owns the rights to the image or content you share, they can sue you for using it without permission.

Do not ever find a random picture on Google (or another blog) and include it in a post of your own. That's a surefire recipe for a lawsuit. Or, at the minimum, a takedown notice requiring you to remove the content.

Here are some tips to always staying on the right side of copyright laws:

1. If you want to include an image from another blog post in a round-up, ask permission. A round-up post is where you write a single post that links to a collection of related articles written by other bloggers. Round-ups are a great way to build relationships with bloggers in your niche. You can also check to see if there's a

policy about sharing on the other website(s). Many have detailed instructions covering what you can and cannot use.

2. Don't ever plagiarize. Create original content instead of stealing it from others.

3. If someone inspired you, give them credit and a link back to their site.

4. Don't use songs you don't have permission to use in any video content.

5. Use your own images or images that are clearly available for use commercially. Read the fine print of every image you want to use.

6. Don't change images (adding filters, editing it, etc.) unless you have permission to do so.

LIST BUILDING

Did you survive the legal section? I know it's a lot of information, but you will want to get your blog started the right way. Email lists are another way to do that. Email lists are gold.

You see, social media networks are always changing their algorithms. The people who like your page on Facebook might not actually see any of the content you post. It's the same with all the other networks. You don't own them, and you don't have any say in changes that happen.

What you do own, however, is your email list. It's your direct line to your readers. And it's extremely valuable. Don't ever take your list for granted or use the email addresses you've been entrusted with for shady purposes.

Before you can start collecting email addresses, there are a couple of things you'll need:

1. An email service provider.

2. A form for your readers to use to enter their email address.

Let's start with the first one.

EMAIL SERVICE PROVIDERS (ESPS)

In order to comply with the CAN-SPAM act, you can't mass email people your blog's newsletters from your personal email address. There are legal requirements you must meet, including providing an option for unsubscribing, displaying your business address, and identifying your business as the sender. You also need permission to send emails to people. Having them opt in to your email newsletter is how they give you that permission.

There are plenty of ESPs out there. Here are five of the most popular for bloggers:

> MailChimp
> MailerLite
> Mad Mimi
> ConvertKit
> AWeber

Some email service providers are free up to a certain number of subscribers, and others start as a paid service. If you are bootstrapping your blog, select a free provider to start.

I started with MailChimp, because it was free. However, I quickly moved to a paid ConvertKit plan because the features I wanted were not included in the free MailChimp plan at the time.

I love ConvertKit and have been using their service for over two years. Even though my list is small enough that I would still qualify for free plans with some providers, I love the quality of ConvertKit. For me, it's worth paying a small fee every month.

However, there are bloggers who love MailerLite. And AWeber. And Mad Mimi. And MailChimp. And other ESPs. You can find plenty of detailed reviews on all of these (and more) online. If you find one you're interested in, learn all you can. Here are some of the available features to keep in mind as you read reviews and shop around:

Multiple Opt-In Offers

If you plan to offer multiple freebies (covered below) to your readers, you need to make sure your plan makes it easy to do so, without requiring you to build a complete new list for each.

Ease of Use

Some ESPs are intuitive. They're drag and drop, and you don't have to worry about your design skills when you sit down to email your list. Others take a bit more effort. However, once you learn how to do it, you should be able to keep doing it going forward.

There's a learning curve regardless of the ESP you select. You must decide how much time you're willing to devote to learning the system.

List Segmentation

If you talk about multiple topics on your blog, some people may want to hear about one topic and not another. Or you might want to send a follow-up email to everyone who downloaded a certain opt-in from you, but not to anyone else.

This is segmenting your list. You break your whole list into separate groups based on criteria of your choice. Some bloggers don't want to segment their list. And that's okay. I rarely segment mine. But if you want to, make sure your ESP makes it easy for you.

Autoresponders

When you subscribe to a freebie, it often triggers a series of emails from a blogger. These are meant to provide engagement and education. They range from a single email to a sequence of twenty or more.

These emails are sent to everyone who subscribes, but the blogger isn't sitting there manually hitting send at the right time. That'd be too hard to do! Instead, email service providers allow you to automate this process with autoresponders. Autoresponders happen automatically when triggered. They allow you to set it and forget it when it comes to many of your emails.

Price

Always look at the price you will need to pay and learn what's included in that price. For instance, ConvertKit has a couple of pricing tiers available. The number of people on your list dictates which tier you are in. So, if your list size increases past the threshold of your current tier, you'll start paying the higher amount.

Some providers are free until you reach a certain subscriber count. Others offer a basic free plan, but you can't use all the features.

Don't feel obligated to pay for a service you can't afford just because other bloggers are using it. Free is a great place to start, as long as the free plan provides all the features you need.

Remember, you can always upgrade or switch later. When I switched from MailChimp to ConvertKit, I was worried it'd be a hassle. It was not. There were great step-by-step tutorials, and the entire process took about ten minutes.

Reporting Tools

If you don't look at data about your emails, you won't know if your current strategy works. At a minimum you need to know what percentage of your emails are being opened, and which links are getting clicks. This will help you tailor your emails to give your readers more of what they want. You can use this information to look for patterns. Are there certain subject lines you use that get more opens than others?

You will also want to know who isn't opening your emails. After not reading any of your emails for a while, a subscriber becomes a cold subscriber.

If you are in a higher pricing tier and many of your subscribers are cold, you want to have the ability to drop them from your list. That way you aren't paying for someone who doesn't want to hear from you anymore.

Customer Support

Problems happen. When they happen, you need to know what support options you are entitled to. Some companies offer great support for all users. Others offer better options to paid users.

Make sure you know what you can do when you run into trouble. Check out the documentation available for users. You need access to the directions for how to do common tasks with your service.

Availability of Forms

Without forms, no one will ever get on your email list. You need a form to capture their name and email address.

Some ESPs make it easy to add forms to WordPress. They integrate well. Others do not. If your service doesn't integrate with your form, you'll need to manually add people to your list. And that's a task a busy blogger can sometimes forget to do.

Before signing up with a provider, find out what works for collecting email address with that service. Ask other bloggers, look for reviews, or read the documentation. You should put a couple of sign-up forms on your blog. I currently have forms on my:

> Home page

> About page

> Blog posts

By having multiple forms available, you give readers multiple chances to sign up without making them search. Most readers are busy and won't bother to search. By making it easy for them, you'll get more subscribers.

EMAIL FREEBIES

A freebie entices a reader to hand over their email address. It's a small gift you give in exchange for their information. Here are some common freebies:

> A short, free course

> An ebook

> A printable workbook, worksheet, or checklist

> A sample of your paid product (like five free stock photos or a single lesson from your paid course)

> Video content

Take some time to brainstorm potential freebies. You want your freebie to meet these four criteria:

1. Relevant to your content (don't use a meal planner freebie if you never talk about meal planning)

2. Useful and solves a problem for your reader

3. Easy to access and utilize

4. High quality

Think about what kind of freebie you want to offer. Spend some time brainstorming. Then, pick one and go with it. You will learn more going through the process of creating your first freebie than you can by simply reading about it. Making the freebie will help you get a sense of the process. It might be difficult the first time, but each new offer you create will be easier.

In the next section, I will explain how to create a simple downloadable freebie.

HOW TO CREATE A FREEBIE

The program I use to create the freebie depends on the kind I'm trying to make. If it's mainly a text-based document, like an ebook, I use Word. I already know how to use it, and I can add borders and pictures. When the document looks good, I save it as a PDF.

If I'm making an image-heavy freebie, such as a resource guide, I use an online tool called Canva. While there are paid options available, the free version of Canva has worked well for me so far.

In Canva, I select the "Presentation" template. After I find one I like, it takes a little time to switch out the pre-loaded content for my own materials. I like Canva because I don't have to worry about design. The templates keep it simple. There's also a PDF option when saving.

Once your freebie is done, get another person to look at it. I typically ask my husband or one of my sisters to proof it for me. I use their recommendations for content and design to make any changes, then I save it as a PDF again.

HOW TO GET YOUR FREEBIE TO YOUR READERS

When your freebie is ready, you need to put it to use. The exact steps you follow depend on your ESP. Be sure to check their documentation.

Here's a quick overview of the process.

1. Create a form for your freebie (include a screenshot so people know what they'll get).

2. Upload your freebie to the incentive email your readers receive after signing up.

3. Embed your form on your website.

That's it! When people see the form promoting your offer, they can decide if they want it or not. If they do, they enter their email address and hit enter. The email arrives automatically, delivering the freebie to them.

A FEW POSTS

Before sending people to your blog, you need to have a couple of posts published. This way they will have something to read once they get there.

If you have multiple categories on your blog, consider writing one in each category before launching. This gives your readers a better idea the type of content they'll find.

It also helps if you have several weeks' worth of content scheduled. This way you can focus on launching and marketing, without having to worry about publishing on time. I will walk you through exactly how to create and schedule a blog post in the next chapter.

IMAGES FOR SHARING

Visual content gets shared on social media. If you don't add these elements to your blog posts, you won't see many shares.

For every blog post, you need a minimum of two images. The first is the cover image. This is typically a wide rectangular shape, like a banner, and it's perfect for sharing on Facebook and Twitter. The second is a Pinnable image. These are long rectangles with easy to read text.

You can add more images if you enjoy it and have time. Some bloggers optimize one photo at the dimensions for Twitter, and one for Facebook.

I use Canva and PicMonkey to prepare images for my posts. If I'm working on my smartphone, the Canva app is perfect for creating images on the go. If I'm on my computer, I use Canva for cover images and PicMonkey to create pins.

Some bloggers use PowerPoint to create a template for pictures. Others use Photoshop. I recommend trying a couple of programs and sticking with one that's easy for you to use. It's best to start with a template and customize it to fit your content.

Another option is to hire a designer to create images for you. I've done this when I was short on time and had a little extra money.

You need to use high quality photos for your images. Ideally, you'd take these yourself. But if that isn't a possibility, you can use stock photos. There are some stock photos you pay for, and others you can use freely.

As mentioned earlier, always verify the copyright on images. You can get in serious trouble (and fined) for using photos without permission.

To locate free stock images, I typically use the following sites:

> Pexels
> Unsplash
> Pixabay

There are also plenty of photographers who offer free stock photos as a bonus to people who sign up for their newsletters. Here are a couple of suggestions for you:

> Haute Stock
> Pixistock
> Dabbles & Babbles

A BRAND

You want readers to see your images and know they are from you. You do this by branding your images.

Branding can be as simple as adding your domain to your images. You might also have a couple of colors you use exclusively. Or a specific font combination.

On your blog, you will want your brand to include a logo. You can use this logo on your social media images, or you can include your blog's name and URL.

It is important to understand that branding can become a stopping point for bloggers. They so badly want to nail the branding they completely stop doing anything else until it's perfect.

Don't let the fear of less-than-perfect branding keep you from making progress with your dream of running a profitable blog. Pick something to start with and use it for a while, then tweak what isn't working or change it up completely.

A QUICK WAY FOR USERS TO SHARE CONTENT

It's frustrating as a reader to discover a great post and want to share it, but to have no easy options available. Yes, your readers can copy and paste the link. However, that's an extra step many people won't bother with.

Make it easy for your readers to share by having the Pinterest PinIt Button and Jetpack plugins (or something similar) mentioned in chapter two installed and activated. Then configure the plugins for social shares.

Doing this allows readers to easily Pin content, give it a Tweet, or a share it on Facebook. And if you make it easy for your readers to share, they're more likely to do so.

There are several styles of share buttons available. You can pick buttons that float along with your content as readers scroll, or buttons that are static. The style you use depends on your personal preference, and most importantly, on your readers' preferences.

SET UP SOCIAL ACCOUNTS FOR YOUR BLOG

Now is the time to set up social accounts for your blog. Sign up for them on any platform you currently use or think you may use in the future. This way you can get a similar username across all networks.

However, just because you sign up for an account doesn't mean you need to use it right now. Social media quickly becomes a time suck. And if you're trying to jump into every platform simultaneously, it will overwhelm you.

Pick one or two to focus on right now. I recommend starting with Pinterest and Facebook, but if your audience isn't on those platforms, pick the ones where they are. You need to be where your ideal reader is.

Once you get a solid social media plan in place for your first one or two, and are feeling comfortable, consider adding another one. You'll get much more traction this way than if you just dabble in all of them.

Chapter six goes into more detail on social media marketing and provides information on how to set up the accounts.

ACTION STEPS

1. Create an about page for your blog.

2. Create a contact page for your blog.

3. Create a disclosure page for your blog.

4. Add a privacy policy.

5. Select an email service provider to use (I recommend MailerLite for a free option, and ConvertKit as a paid one).

6. Brainstorm and create a freebie, then connect it to your ESP.

7. Decide how to brand your images.

8. Ensure your social share buttons are configured and enabled.

You are making great progress on your blog. Now it's time to learn how to craft blog posts that your ideal readers can't wait to share. Chapter five is all about creating content for your blog.

CHAPTER FIVE

Create Content

Now that you have a solid foundation, it's time to write. This chapter will help you turn your ideas into shareable blog posts.

If you've never written a blog post before, it's important to spend a few minutes becoming familiar with this form of writing.

When I started blogging, my writing experience was all academic. Academic writing calls for three to five sentences in each paragraph. Long sentences are encouraged, especially if they use lots of academic vocabulary. Writing without personality is just fine.

I was used to writing this way, and my early blog posts would have earned an A in an English class. The problem? Blog posts aren't supposed to follow an academic mold. They have their own format.

Here are six key features of great blog posts. They:

1. Are easy to scan and read quickly.
2. Have images.
3. Have a clear purpose.
4. Use a conversational tone.
5. Have short paragraphs.
6. Provide helpful links.

If you aren't used to writing for the web, these will help you. Let's look at each feature in more detail.

#1: SCANNABLE

Online readers don't have a great attention span. Instead of reading your post word for word, almost all your readers will scan it first. If you catch their attention and they like what they see, they might go back and read it.

Because of this, you need to make sure your post is easily scannable. Your goal is to get rid of long blocks of text. You can do this with:
> Bullet points
> Numbered lists
> Subheadings
Break up the text and make it easy for readers to tell what your post is about.

#2: IMAGES

I covered images in chapter four, but I'll reiterate their importance here. Put high-quality images in your blog posts. Images break up your text and make the content more shareable.

#3: CLEAR PURPOSE

Why are you writing a blog post? Before you put any words on paper, you need to have a clear purpose. Start by knowing what your readers will get out of your post. Then do the actual writing. This will help you stay on topic.

#4: CONVERSATIONAL TONE

Your readers want to hear your voice—not a professor's voice, or a robot's. You should write a blog post like you're sitting down with a friend talking over a cup of cocoa.

I must admit, this is the part of writing blog posts I struggle with the most. I spent so much time writing without my voice that it took me a while to find it.

One strategy that helped me was to read each post aloud. This shows me whether it sounds like something I'd actually say. If it doesn't, I know I still have some polishing to do.

You can also think of a person you know who fits your ideal reader persona. What would you write to this specific person?

#5: SHORT PARAGRAPHS

In school, you may have been taught to use three to five sentences in every single paragraph. But to keep your post flowing and scannable, your paragraphs need to be shorter.

How short?

Sometimes a single sentence will do.

Other times you need more. And you might even use more than five sentences in a paragraph, especially if your sentences are short. Like this one. It really depends on what you write about and how well the ideas flow together. If you think it's time for a break, end your paragraph.

#6: HELPFUL LINKS

Providing links in your posts helps your reader to learn more about the topic. In a single blog post, you may link to:

> Other blog posts on your site

> Blog posts on different websites

> Resources (such as books, tools, etc.)

Interlinking (including a link to more of your content) promotes your content and builds a strong site. It keeps your readers on your website for longer and increases the likelihood that they sign up for your email list.

If you link to another website, be sure it's one you trust. You don't want to send your readers to an unreliable site, or worse, one full of spam.

When you link, use anchor text. Instead of having a link visible, such as sallyannmiller.com, you will provide the link within a word or phrase, like this: *Check out Sally's website for more information on making money from home.*

You can add links in Word, Google Docs, or the WordPress editor. Simply highlight the word(s) you want to use. Then, click either the link button (the icon looks like two links of a chain), or insert hyperlink.

You will see a space to add the web address. Make sure you type it correctly and include the whole thing. To avoid mistakes, open the page you want to link to and then copy the URL from the address line in your Internet browser.

EMAILS ASKING FOR LINKS

At some point in your blogging career, you'll likely receive an email asking you to include a link. It'll read something like this:

> *Hey, blogger!*
> *I just read your post (post name). I wrote a post on a similar topic. I'd love for you to link to my post in yours. It'll give your readers useful information.*
> *Let me know if you want to hear more about my post.*
> *Name*

Do not feel obligated to provide the link. These people are trying to get more links to their sites. These links help their ranking in Google. But giving this link isn't helpful for you, or your blog.

You must decide what you want to do. If you don't already know and trust the person who is reaching out to you, I recommend declining. This helps prevent you from accidentally linking to any unscrupulous sites. You can either ignore them or email back and decline.

Ignoring them will likely result in a couple of automatic follow-up emails. Link hunters are persistent!

THE WRITING PROCESS

You need to decide where you are going to draft your posts. Here are three popular options:

1. WordPress: You can type directly into the WordPress editor. That's where I draft most of my posts. But if something goes wrong, you risk losing everything. Save frequently. If your computer crashes, be sure to check your drafts section on WordPress before you panic.

2. Word: You can write directly in Word, like any other document. The spell checker is solid here, and you can often spot errors you might miss in another program. However, your formatting may not transfer correctly into WordPress if you simply copy and paste it. This means you'll need to spend a little extra time preparing your post for publication.

3. Google Docs: When I write blog posts for clients, they almost always want it submitted as a Google Doc. Copying and pasting into WordPress will keep the formatting.

Now that you know what blog posts should look like, you are ready to write some. I've found the fastest way to do this is to follow a writing process. There are four steps in the writing process:

1. Outline your post.
2. Research your idea.
3. Draft your post.
4. Edit your post.

And remember, the more you write, the faster you will get. Don't be surprised if your first blog post takes hours to compose. You will get better and more comfortable over time.

STEP ONE: OUTLINE YOUR POST

I used to argue with my English teachers in high school about outlines. I didn't see the point. I thought they were just a waste of time. Whenever one was required, I wrote it after I drafted my paper.

However, as a blogger, I finally realized the point of an outline. They make the writing process easier. Instead of trying to figure out the direction while you write, you can take care of it before you start. Outlines are your map for your blog post. An outline helps you to plan the beginning, the end, and major landmarks between the two.

Knowing where you are going is beneficial, especially when you're trying to write while your kids are interrupting your work. Having a basic outline will help get your mind back on track each time you find time to write.

Here are the steps to make an outline:

1. Read through your headlines and pick one you feel like writing about.

2. Write your headline at the top of the page.

3. Think about what you want to tell your reader. What is the point of this blog post?

4. Write down any subheadings that come to mind. These are your main points.

5. Can you divide any of your subheadings further? Write down the possibilities.

6. Look over your outline and see if everything is on topic. Are there any subheadings that need to be rearranged to make sense?

7. If you have a number in your title, make sure you have the correct number of points.

Your basic outline is now complete and you can move on to the research phase.

STEP TWO: RESEARCH YOUR IDEA

You don't need to do tons of research for each post. But you do need to figure out which links you want to include. By taking time to find these now, you will avoid getting sucked into the Internet while you're drafting your post. It will save you time in the long run.

Copy and paste any links into your outline, in the section in which you plan to use them. This way you can easily grab them when you are ready.

> *Don't ever take someone's words and try to pass them off as your own. This is stealing, and it's not right.*

Likewise, you don't want to copy someone else's outline. Make it your own. Your readers want to hear you, not a regurgitated version of someone else.

On a similar note, cite your sources. If you include statistics, provide a link where your readers can check out the data for themselves.

> *There's nothing new under the sun.*

Whatever topic you plan to write about, it's probable other bloggers have already covered it. You aren't likely to come up with an idea that's completely unique and has never been done.

Your job is to put your own spin on the topic. Even if thousands of other bloggers have already covered it, you can bring something new to the subject. You can bring your own experience, stories, and perspectives. That is different. It's you that separates you from all the other bloggers out there.

STEP THREE: DRAFT YOUR POST

With an outline in place and your research done, it's time to draft. Use your outline as a guide. In general, an outline has three parts: an introduction, the main points, and a conclusion.

The introduction is often the hardest for me to come up with, so I skip it at first. After everything else is done, I go back to the top and write the introduction. If you can't think of how to begin, I highly recommend this method.

Your introduction should catch your reader's attention. Here are five suggestions for how to start each post:

> Ask a question

> Share a story

> Share a quote (with credit given, of course)

> Present a statistic

> Let loose with a bit of your personality

You want your introduction to draw your reader in. But since it's the hook to the rest of your post, it should be relevant to the topic.

After a compelling introduction, it's time to work on the main points. For each section, write down what your readers need to know. Focus on getting your ideas down for now. You will go back and edit later, so it doesn't need to be perfect.

If a section gives you trouble, skip it. You can either go back and fill it in or decide to delete it altogether.

When you are finished with your main points, it's time to wrap up your blog post. A conclusion is a brief way to tie it all together. This is also where you will include your call to action.

What do you want your readers to do after reading your post? Do you want them to share it with their friends? Or add a comment? Perhaps you want them to check out a product.

Think about your post. Then pick *one* call to action and include it at the end of your post. By limiting it to one, you aren't asking your readers to make a choice. A single option makes it easy for them to know what to do.

Here are some example calls to action:

> **Leave a Comment:** Have you read any of these books? I'd love for you to share your opinions in the comments below.

> **Share:** If you enjoyed this post, please share it.

> **Subscribe:** Interested in more homemaking tips? Subscribe today to get them delivered straight to your inbox.

> **Check out a Paid Product:** For even more tips on making money from home, check out Sally's other books in the Paid to Stay Home series.

STEP FOUR: EDIT YOUR POST

Once your draft is done, save it and walk away. You need to clear your head and give yourself some space before editing. Otherwise you risk missing errors.

When you're ready to edit, read your post aloud. If you read silently, your brain can sometimes trick you. Instead of reading what you wrote, you might read what you meant to write.

By reading the post out loud, word for word, your ears notice errors your eyes might have missed. As you read, look for:

> Fluff: Get rid of extra, unnecessary words.

> Jargon: You don't want tons of unfamiliar terms in your posts.

> Areas that don't make sense: Do you need to add something to clarify a point?

> Difficulty with organization: Now is the time to rearrange if needed.

> Repetition: You only need to state something once.

> Errors in grammar or spelling.

Make the changes you find, and then read it aloud again. If possible, get someone else to read it for you. I often have either my husband or our teen read my posts.

Once you have your post in decent shape, here's a tip to make it even better. Copy and paste it into the free Hemingway App. This editor helps you improve your writing. With color coded highlighting, it points out overly complex sentences and common errors. Work through the suggestions, and your post will be ready for readers.

PUBLISH YOUR POST IN WORDPRESS

Before readers can see your post, you must publish it with WordPress. Here are directions for doing that.

1. Log into your WordPress account.
2. Click on "Add New" at the top. From there, select blog post.
3. In the text editor, copy and paste your post.
4. Double check your formatting. On the right-hand side, select "Preview." Your post will open in a new tab, and this is what your readers will see.
5. Make sure your subheadings are in H2 or H3 instead of just in bold.
6. Click on your links and make sure they work.
7. Set the featured image from the option on the right-hand side. Once you click the button, select "upload file" then "set as featured image."
8. Add any other images to the body of the post by selecting "Add Media." Then upload the pictures and insert them into the post.
9. Preview your post once more to verify the images.
10. If you want to publish the post immediately, hit "Publish."
11. If you want to schedule your post, select the date and time from the right-hand side. Then hit "Schedule."

ACTION STEPS

1. Pick the headline you want to use for your post.
2. Outline your post.
3. Complete any research.
4. Draft your post.
5. Edit your post, making sure it's in blog format.
6. Use the Hemingway App to help with proofreading.
7. Get your post into WordPress and either schedule it or publish it.
8. Celebrate writing your first blog post.
9. Repeat for additional posts.

Crafting great blog posts takes time. It's helpful to create a content checklist. This ensures you don't forget any steps, such as including appropriate links or keywords.

You are making great progress on your blog. You have your foundation in place and know how to create quality content. You're ready for readers. In the next chapter, I will show you how to start attracting readers to your blog. Let's drive some traffic.

CHAPTER SIX

Market Your Content

Y ou can spend hours creating the perfect blog post. But if you don't spread the word about it, no one will read it. Readers don't magically appear on your blog, eagerly awaiting your every word. You have to tell them why they should visit your website.

And you can't make a single social media post linking to your article and consider yourself done. One link on social media isn't going to send many readers to your blog post. I made this mistake, and my blog (and income) suffered as a result.

Back in 2016, I needed 15 college credits to keep my teaching credentials current. So, I signed up for three classes in the fall semester. My already hectic schedule went straight to crazy trying to fit in a full-time college load.

In desperation, I cut what I believed were unimportant tasks, like marketing. During this time, I continued to post to my blog once a week. And one of my plug-ins automatically sent out a tweet and a Facebook page update.

That was it. My entire marketing plan for an entire quarter revolved around a single set of automatic shares on each post. I'm sure you know where this story is going. My page views tanked. I had no measurable traffic.

Looking back, I should have cut my blogging schedule in half. By writing only two posts a month, I would have had time to invest in marketing.

Since I can't go back in time and fix my own mistake, I hope I can stress the importance of marketing to you. Learn from what I did and make marketing a priority right from the start. Even if it means publishing fewer blog posts, the long-term results are worth it.

FIGHTING THE MARKETING OVERWHELM

You have tons of options for marketing your blog on social media. In fact, there are so many options it's easy to feel overwhelmed. One expert tells you to do this. Another tells you to never do that. You can find contradicting opinions on every single marketing strategy.

> *How do you cut through information overload and figure out what works? You stop reading about marketing, and you start doing.*

You must learn what works for your audience, and no expert has the perfect formula for you. When you first start marketing your blog, pick two strategies to focus on. Remember creating your ideal reader back in chapter one? What platforms are your readers on daily? That's where you want to start.

Once you're comfortable with one platform, move to another. By taking it slowly, you won't feel overwhelmed.

MARKETING IS NOT ALL ABOUT YOU

Before you market your content, you need to understand the point of marketing. Marketing is not to tell everyone how great you are. It's not to toot your own horn or turn you into a sleazy salesperson.

It's to share what you create with people who can benefit from it and to build relationships and make connections.

When you look at marketing that way, it becomes easier.

Also, remember that you are not the only person who can solve your readers' problems. But you are the best one to solve some specific problems.

There's other content out there your readers would benefit from. And part of your marketing strategy should be to share that content, too. By sharing content other people create, you help increase your chances of success. You show your readers it's not all about you. And you begin building relationships with other bloggers.

When you put together your posts for social media, look for other content your readers will enjoy. This is known as curating content. We'll cover that in more detail later.

In the next few sections, I walk you through the basics of four popular platforms many bloggers use.

PINTEREST FOR BUSINESS

Pinterest is my top source of traffic. It is for many other bloggers as well. But there's something important you need to realize about Pinterest. I mentioned this briefly in chapter three, but it's time for a reminder.

Pinterest is not really a social media network. It's a search engine. And you need a plan to make Pinterest work for you.

Pinterest is all about the visual. So, make sure every single blog post has a Pinnable image. Review the guidelines in chapter four. Even if you aren't focusing on Pinterest right now, include this image. That way your readers can Pin your post if they want to.

You also want to create a Pinterest business account. You can either convert your personal page to a business account or start over with a new one.

Next, you want to enable rich pins. If you browse through your Pinterest feed, you might notice some pins show who pinned them, and some don't. Pins that show this information have a little circular picture at the bottom, and the name of the pinner. These are rich pins.

You need to set up rich pins for your account. Here's a simple way to do it.

Once you're logged into your blog, ensure the YoastSEO plugin is activated. If it is, use the sidebar on the left-hand side to access the social section of Yoast.

From there, click on Facebook. Make sure the "add open graph meta data" option is enabled. This adds important information to your site's head section that Pinterest needs to verify.

Now, log into your Pinterest account, and navigate to the Rich Pin Validator. Enter the URL of a post from your blog in the box, follow the directions on the site, and click on validate.

Once you receive notification of your site's validation, you need to apply for rich pins. Follow the directions on Pinterest and expect an email within a couple of days.

YOUR PINTEREST BOARDS

After your business account is set up, it's time to make sure your boards are ready for viewers. If you're converting a personal account, review all your existing boards.

Will your audience be interested in them? If not, change them to secret. That way you can still see your pins, but your viewers will not.

If you need to create boards, think about what interests your readers. Use clear, concise labels for your boards. This keeps people from having to guess what your boards include.

Try to have at least ten boards for your account. If you're having trouble, brainstorm topics your readers might search for.

One of your boards needs to be dedicated to your blog. You can call this the "Best of (blog name)" board. This is the board where you initially pin all your blog posts.

Make sure you enter descriptions for your boards, using keywords. Also take the time to categorize them. This helps other pinners find your boards.

Take some time to add at least a couple of pins to each of your boards. Do a search for topics that are a good fit. When you see a pin you want to add, be sure to click through to the article first. This way you can make sure the post exists and the link isn't broken.

Taking time to do this helps your followers learn to trust the content you save. It helps stop the spread of pins leading to 404 pages (not found).

If everything looks good, click the "save" button. Select the board you want to pin to and add a description if you want. This is where you can enter keywords, or any comments you have about the post.

GROUP BOARDS

On Pinterest, your boards are yours. You get to decide what pins go into them.

Group boards are different. Group boards have an owner who opens the board up to collaborators. Collaborators then pin content to the board.

Group boards can be a good source of traffic. If you have a small following on Pinterest, but are pinning to a large group board, more people will see your content.

To join a group board, you need to follow the directions the owner set up. These often include following the owner and agreeing to pin only relevant boards.

Always follow the rules. If you need to pin something from the group for every pin you save, then do that. Collaboration is an important part of marketing!

MANUAL PINNING & SCHEDULERS

Manual pinning means you log into Pinterest and click on the "save" button yourself. If you don't have money to spend on a scheduler right now, keep manually pinning. Try to pin at least five pins every day.

Tailwind and BoardBooster are the most popular schedulers. The basic premise is to collect a bunch of relevant pins in advance and assign them to boards. Instead of posting them to your Pinterest account right away, your scheduler hangs onto them. Then, it slowly drips out your saved pins throughout the week or month.

This cuts down the amount of time you need to spend on Pinterest. Though, to help keep your account active, you should continue to do a little manual pinning.

BoardBooster and Tailwind also both have a tribe feature. Tribes are a group of pinners with similar niches. You upload some of your pins to the tribe, and the other members pin them. You then pin their content.

If you join a tribe, be sure to read the rules clearly and follow them. If you need to pin three pins a day, make sure you do your part. Tribes only work if everyone plays along.

I personally prefer BoardBooster, but many bloggers love Tailwind. If you are interested in either, I recommend signing up for a free trial of each. That's what I did.

Then I explored the features of each and decided which one worked better for my personality and budget.

HOW TO GET FOLLOWERS ON PINTEREST

When starting out on Pinterest, you may want to invest some effort in getting followers. However, many social media experts claim that your number of followers has minimal impact on your Pinterest success. For the most part, your number of followers is a vanity metric.

Having said that, here're four ways to increase your followers on Pinterest:

> Share your profile in follow feeds in Facebook Groups.

> Follow influencers in your niche, and their followers.
> Post a link to your profile on your other social profiles.
> Have a Pinterest follow button on your blog.

FACEBOOK BASICS

Tons of people use Facebook. If your target audience hangs out there, make sure you have a Facebook page for your blog.

A Facebook page is not the same as your profile. When you signed up for your personal Facebook account, you created a personal profile. This is where most people connect with their friends and family.

While some bloggers opt to create a second Facebook profile to use for their blog, this violates Facebook terms and conditions. Anyone using a profile to represent a business can lose their account.

It's not a risk I recommend taking. Of course, you can connect with other bloggers on your personal profile. They will just see all the cute cousin pictures and grandma comments you engage with.

Your personal profile can create a business page. This is what you need for your blog. Your page distinguishes that your blog is a business and helps people find you. It's a place where you can control the content and ensure everything is on message for your ideal reader.

Facebook Pages give you insights into your analytics. You can see demographics of people engaging with your posts and use this information to help you create content tailored for your audience. Having a business page also allows you to create ads, once you are ready for some paid marketing.

Finally, there are Facebook Groups. You can start a Facebook Group for your blog. And you can join other groups to help you meet other bloggers and grow your traffic. I cover these in more detail in just a bit.

HOW TO SET UP A FACEBOOK PAGE

To market your blog on Facebook, you need a page. Here's how to create one.

Log into Facebook and select "Pages" from the left-hand menu. At the top of the page, click "Create a Page."

Look at all the options and decide which one is the best fit. Many bloggers go with "Brand or Product."

Next, pick a category. Often bloggers use "Website," but pick the one you think is the best fit.

Enter the name of your blog and click "Get Started."

Now you can customize your page by adding a profile image and a cover image. Many bloggers use their logo for the cover image, and a personal photo for the profile picture. Use images you think best represent your brand.

Once your page is set up, you can access it from your personal profile. It's listed in your Pages section. If you make it a favorite, you also make it easier to access.

WHAT TO SHARE ON FACEBOOK

Facebook is a great place to share every blog post you publish. You can post:
> Behind-the-scenes glimpses of running your business.
> Relevant quotes.
> Posts from other bloggers your audience would like.
> Questions and answers about your niche.
> Polls created with your audience in mind.
> Tips your audience would appreciate.
> Relevant memes.
The most important question to ask yourself before posting anything is:

Will my audience benefit from this?

If the answer is yes, post. If the answer is no, or I'm not sure, then hold off.

HOW TO GROW YOUR FACEBOOK FOLLOWING

You want people to like and follow your Facebook page. Having more followers on Facebook increases the reach of your posts. To help achieve this goal, try the following:

1. Invite your friends to like your page.

2. Join Facebook groups relevant to your niche and participate in social media follow threads.

3. Include a Facebook follow button on your blog.

4. Share some of your blog's content to your personal profile.

5. Post your Facebook page on your other social media sites occasionally and ask your followers to join you on Facebook.

FACEBOOK GROUPS

Facebook Groups allow people with common interests to communicate with each other within a closed space. Facebook Groups are a powerful way to connect with other bloggers and grow your blog.

They can turn into a time suck if you aren't careful. So, before you join a group, carefully read its description, and ask yourself the following questions:

> Am I in the target demographic for this group?

> Are the threads in this group going to benefit me?

> Do I have the time to participate in this group regularly?

> Why do I want to join this group? (What's your goal?)

When you're ready to join, make sure you meet the requirements. Then click the "Join Group" button. Answer any questions the group owner has and wait to find out whether you have been approved.

Once approved, you can begin posting in the group. Make sure you follow the rules. If you can introduce yourself, take the time to do so. Include a link to your blog only if it's allowed.

Don't promote yourself unless it's an approved day or time. You don't want to spam the group. Unauthorized self-promotion often leads to removal from a group.

When you follow the rules, you can make some amazing connections in Facebook Groups. Participate in the threads and promote your blog or social media profiles when allowed.

If you stop enjoying a particular group, or don't see any benefit from it, you can always leave. You aren't stuck in it forever.

TWITTER BASICS

Are you on Twitter? If you enjoy Tweeting, and your audience is there, this can be a fun way to grow your blog. Here's a bit of information about Twitter.

Slightly more males than females use Twitter regularly. It's a platform where brevity wins, with a 280-character limit on all Tweets (it used to be 140, but they changed it in fall of 2017). It's also a place to break out your hashtags. #bloggingtips

Previously known as the pound sign, hashtags allow people to track content about a specific topic. So, if you want to find information about a topic on Twitter, you can do a hashtag search. Your results include all sorts of content with that particular hashtag.

By using hashtags, you can draw your audience to you on Twitter. You can use hashtags to search for other bloggers in your niche. If others who write about similar topics are finding success on Twitter, that means your audience is on there.

HOW TO SET UP A TWITTER ACCOUNT

Setting up a Twitter account for your blog takes just a few minutes. You need to pick a handle. This is what goes after the @ sign when someone wants to find you on Twitter.

You have limited characters, so you may need to get creative. If the name you want is unavailable, think of a different one.

Once you have your account, add a picture. Try to use a personal photo instead of your logo. This helps provide a more personal touch and draw in readers.

Now it's time to write your bio. Tell other people who you are and what you're about. You only have a few characters to do it with, so choose every word carefully.

Make it interesting. Throw in some personal hobbies or a fun fact. Users want to connect with interesting people.

Also, make sure to put your blog's URL in your profile. That way people know where to find you.

START FOLLOWING PEOPLE & TWEETING

Start following other people on Twitter. You can begin with influencers in your niche and other bloggers. As you make more connections, follow those people on Twitter.

Next, it's time to Tweet. Twitter recently increased its character limit on tweets, so you can fit some more words in there. But Twitter is the place for sharing short thoughts and bits of content, not huge paragraphs.

In your tweets, include a couple of relevant hashtags. Then, when people are searching for that hashtag, they might find your tweet and click through to see what you wrote. Hashtags tell others what you're talking about and help connect people interested in the same topics.

Wondering what to tweet? Here are some suggestions:

> Sharable quotes from each of your blog posts
> A link to each blog post you publish with a brief overview
> Content from other people
> Quick updates about your life
> Fun facts

On Twitter you can retweet content by clicking on the "Retweet" button. This shares a tweet from another user with your audience.

Retweeting is an effective way to make connections on Twitter. When you retweet something, the original poster is notified. You can also like tweets by selecting the heart. This notifies the poster, which can help get your name recognized.

Make sure you only retweet and post content your audience can benefit from.

INSTAGRAM BASICS

Another visual platform, Instagram is a great place to share your content, especially if you are marketing to a younger, female audience. Almost sixty percent of Instagram users are under 30, and almost seventy percent are female.

Setting up an Instagram account is straightforward. After downloading the Instagram app, create an account or log in through Facebook. You want a business account so you can access the analytics.

Put a link to your blog in the website field. This is the only clickable link you get.

Make your bio interesting. It's limited, so use emojis to cut down on characters. Let your personality shine through.

You have to decide if you want to use your personal name or your blog's name for the account. Many bloggers use their name, followed by this symbol | and their blog's name. But, if that combination has too many characters, you may have to be creative.

On Instagram you don't have access to the analytics until you reach 100 followers. Make that your baby step goal. Start following others in your niche, and consistently share useful posts. This encourages people to follow you back.

WHAT TO SHARE ON INSTAGRAM

The content you share on Instagram depends on your niche. A mom blogger's content looks dramatically different than a fashion blogger's.

Pick content that speaks to your ideal readers, and use the caption to share helpful ideas.

You can also share a picture for each blog post. Many bloggers update the link in their profile each time they do this and write "updated link in profile" as part of the caption to encourage viewers to click through and read.

Try creating an image with a quote from your blog post. Or a quote you like in general. Just be sure to give credit where it's due.

I encourage you to share some personal shots, too. Give your readers a behind-the-scenes peek at who you are and what you do.

VIDEO MARKETING BASICS

Video marketing is taking the blogging world by storm. It's available in some form on every platform. If you create videos, your content is more likely to get shared.

But going on camera can feel scary. Especially if you're shy. My advice? Do it scared. The first one is the hardest. Once you post a video, you never have to do your first one again.

Videos aren't meant to be perfect. Don't script them out and read it like a robot. Be yourself and do what you do best—provide useful information to your viewers.

There are two main options with video marketing. Do it live, or prerecord it.

Going live means you won't have a chance to edit it. What you say is what people hear. Many viewers like watching live because of this. It's more real to them, instead of a staged production.

Prerecording makes sense sometimes, though. Especially if you're creating a video series and want to record it all at once. If you do this, upload your videos to

YouTube and share the links when you're ready. Or, if the platform allows, upload the video direct to your social media account.

You don't need fancy equipment to record video. The camera on your smartphone is quality enough to work for most purposes.

You may want to invest in a tripod for your camera, with an adapter to support the camera. This way you don't have to try to balance your phone or constantly hold it.

Then it's a matter of hitting the record button and talking. If you have some talking points beforehand, it helps you speak with more confidence.

Look directly into the lens. Make sure you know where your lens is. Sometimes it's hard to tell on a smartphone. You can always run your finger over your camera and watch the screen. When you block the lens, make note of where it is.

Remember, you are your own special sauce. You are what separates your blog from all the other ones out there. Be yourself, and let your audience see who you are.

DON'T GET OVERWHELMED

This chapter is full of information, and I don't want you to start implementing it all at once. Read it to get a general idea of your options, then pick a platform and dive in.

That platform will feel different at first. It'll take you a while to figure out how it works. Keep trying and soon it'll feel natural. You won't have to think so much about what to share.

When you're comfortable on one platform, add another. Don't try to do it all at once, or you will feel overwhelmed.

No matter what platform you're on, here are some final tips to help you promote your content.

1. Experiment with post styles to see what type of content your followers engage with.

2. Use your data. See which posts are performing and look for patterns. Find out when your users are active and adjust your posting schedule accordingly.

3. Use scheduling tools to help you schedule posts in bulk. This way you aren't glued to social media all day long.

4. Remember to build relationships. Respond to comments and join the conversation on other people's posts when you can.

GUEST POSTING

The goal of marketing is to get your content in front of your ideal readers. Social media isn't the only way to accomplish that goal.

Another marketing strategy is to collaborate with other bloggers to create guest posts. This is when you write a post that another blogger publishes on their blog. Your words are now being read by someone else's audience, which has potential to boost your own blog traffic.

You often receive a bio at the end of your guest post and can include a link back to your blog. This way, readers who are interested can click through and find you. It also gives you an external link to your blog, which is beneficial.

While there are huge sites that offer guest posting opportunities (like Money Saving Mom), you may need to start off with smaller blogs. As you gain more experience, you can work your way up to blogs with lots of readers.

If you're interested in trying the guest post strategy, here are some tips for finding opportunities.

First, make sure the blog you want to post on is related to your niche. You can craft an amazing post and get it in front of lots of people. But if those people aren't your ideal audience, you won't benefit as much from the experience.

Brainstorm a list of blogs with overlapping audiences. Then, start checking out those blogs. See if they have posts from guest bloggers. If they do, read their content. You want to suggest a topic that will fit within the scope of their blog and be beneficial for their readers.

Also, check to see whether they have published any guest posting guidelines. You will need to comply with these when reaching out to the blog owner. When you are ready to contact the blogger, check their contact page for an email address. Then, write your proposal. To increase your chances of not being marked spam, do these things:

> Use the blogger's name (and double check the spelling!)

> Introduce yourself and how you found this blogger.

> Provide some information that shows you know what their blog is about (for instance, I loved your post about _____).

> Ask for a guest post and include information about what you want the post to be about.

> Share why you think this post is the perfect one for their audience and why you are the best person to write it.

> Include your name and blog's name as you close.

> Make sure you comply with their guest posting guidelines, if they have any.

If you don't like the idea of cold pitching bloggers with ideas, here are two other strategies to try.

1. Do a Google search for "Your Niche" + "Guest Posts." Your results will often include blogs with a submission form for bloggers to use to apply for guest posts.

2. Join Facebook Groups that include a Collaboration thread. These often have people asking for guest posts for their blog. Just make sure the blog has at least some readers before you accept. Otherwise you won't get any traction from it.

GET YOUR CONTENT INTO THE WORLD

There are other marketing strategies to get your content out there. For instance, once you are making some money and you have a little to spend on marketing, you can use paid ads across different platforms.

Another way to get your name out in the blogging world is to be interviewed for blog posts or podcasts. Look for bloggers or podcasters who post series of interviews and have an audience made up of your ideal readers. Then, reach out and see if they are looking for guests for their interviews. Be sure to include information about why you are a great candidate.

However you decide to start your marketing journey, make sure you start. Not marketing means you are deciding not to have an income-producing blog. Remember that without readers, you won't make any money.

ACTION STEPS

1. Review your ideal reader from chapter one. What social media platforms are your readers using daily?

2. Pick two of those platforms to begin experimenting with. Create your business accounts and update your bios.

3. Begin creating content to share. Look for sharable quotes from your blog posts.

4. Keep a document of other people's content you'd like to share. Collecting this as you go means you always have something to share.

5. Begin engaging with people on the social media platforms you selected.

6. Make a list of possible blogs you could guest post on, and/or be interviewed for.

Now that you have a plan in place to get your content in front of readers, it's time to switch gears. In the next three chapters, I dive into earning money with your blog. Keep reading to learn how to create a monetization strategy.

CHAPTER SEVEN

Create Your Monetization Strategy

You've made a lot of progress on building the foundation for a profitable blog. It's time to create your monetization strategy. Without this plan, you won't earn money from your blog.

Some monetization strategies you can start immediately. For instance, you can include affiliate links in your posts right from the beginning. You won't earn much (if anything) from them, but it will give you a great chance to practice the strategy and get it refined.

You can offer services from the get-go. You'll have to be more proactive at marketing your services and finding your clients until they start finding you, but this is a good way to get the income needle moving.

Other earning methods require more readers and content. For instance, you can launch a product of your own anytime. But, you won't have anyone buying it unless you have an audience to sell to. Keep working on building your audience, and then dive into this type of monetization.

Don't assume you will need to have thousands of page views each month to make money. Small blogs can earn, too. The secret is to make sure your content is a great fit for your ideal reader. Then they'll keep coming back and you'll build trust. The more your readers trust you, the more likely they are to buy from you. Even if there aren't very many of them.

When monetizing, you must find what works for you and your audience. You might need to experiment with several things. On the plus side, having multiple streams of income is never a bad idea. If one income stream suddenly dries up, you won't lose your entire income.

In this chapter, I will introduce you to six different methods of monetizing your blog. They are:

1. Affiliate marketing
2. Product creation
3. Offering services
4. Advertising income
5. Sponsored posts
6. Hosting events

After the overview in this chapter, I will dive deep into affiliate marketing, product creation and offering services in the next two chapters.

AFFILIATE MARKETING

Affiliate marketing is when you promote a product or service belonging to someone else. When a visitor clicks through your link and makes a purchase, you receive a commission.

When you sign up as an affiliate for a company or brand, you receive an affiliate link. This link has unique identifying characters in it. It's different than all the other affiliate links out there.

Once you have your link, you promote the product. Make sure you use your affiliate link each time to get credit for any sales.

How do you promote your affiliate links? Here are some ideas:

> Write a blog post reviewing the product.

> Compare and contrast two products.

> Write a round-up of five of the best tools (or books, or whatever the product is).

> Promote the product in a tweet.

> Post a Facebook update about the product.

> Create an appealing pin and link it with your affiliate link.

> Do a Facebook Live about the product and include your affiliate link in the comments.

As I mentioned in chapter two, you must disclose any relationship you have with a product or company.

No matter where you post your affiliate link, you must tell your readers that you will benefit from their purchase. In addition to having a full disclosure page on your blog, you need to include a disclosure on every single post that contains an affiliate link.

And this disclosure can't be at the bottom of the post. Before seeing an affiliate link to click on, your readers need to know what it is.

You must also use disclosures on social media. If you have limited characters, you may need to be creative. You can use the hashtags #ad or #afflink to disclose. If you have more space available, be a little more transparent in your disclosure.

HOW MUCH CAN YOU EARN WITH AFFILIATE MARKETING?

Each affiliate program runs a little differently. Some offer a flat fee per sale. Others offer a percentage. You can even find programs that pay you monthly for as long as the customer you referred continues to be a paying client.

Make sure you learn the specifics for each program you are with. This way there are no surprises.

When you first start, you may not get many sales. You may have months where you don't earn any money from your affiliate links. But don't give up. There really is no limit on the amount of money you can earn through affiliate marketing.

Caroline Vencil from CarolineVencil.com regularly shares monthly income reports on her blog. Affiliate marketing is her top source of income. I love how she breaks down this information so readers can see which companies she earns money from.

In October of 2017, Caroline earned $12,007 from her blog. Of that, $7,368 came from affiliate marketing. She broke down all the numbers for you to see here.

Now, you can't just throw a couple of affiliate links online and expect to bring in four figures. It's taken Caroline years to build her blog and her following. Her readers trust her and know they can count on her to deliver quality information. She doesn't take advantage of them by linking to subpar products.

The next chapter dives into affiliate marketing in more detail.

PRODUCT CREATION

Is there a product you can make that would meet the needs of your readers? If so, consider creating it.

When you create your own product, you can sell it for an income. And since you don't have to continue remaking the product each time you sell it, it's a more passive form of income.

Here are five common products bloggers create:

1. Ebooks

2. Downloadable products (workbooks, bookmarks, a PDF game, customizable labels, etc.)

3. Courses

4. A video series

5. An audio-based training series

Each time you sell a product, you receive income. The more products you sell, the more you earn. And by selling multiple products, you diversify your income.

Suzi Whitford from StartaMomBlog.com shares her income reports with her readers. In September of 2017, she earned $24,754. Her courses and ebooks accounted for a large chunk.

Once again, it takes time and consistency for bloggers to earn this kind of money. The first monthly income report Suzi ever published (for June of 2016) was for $1,007. Of that, almost $900 was from one of her products. Back then, she had fewer products available and a much smaller audience.

In chapter nine, I will talk more about how to create and sell a product from your blog.

OFFERING SERVICES

By creating a "Hire Me" page on your website, you have a home base for offering a service. Providing a service is a fast way to monetize your blog even if you have a small following.

Here are ten services you could offer:

1. Freelance writing

2. Virtual assistant work

3. Graphic design

4. Coaching

5. Photography/stock photos

6. Web design

7. Proofreading/editing

8. Social media management

9. Bookkeeping

10. Blog management

Think about what you enjoy doing and what you're good at. What services are people willing to pay for? Then, add a Hire Me page to your website.

Your income from services depends on how much you work, and how much you charge. Most of my income comes from freelance writing and virtual assistant services. I currently average $2,300 a month working on a part-time basis.

Other bloggers earn much more! Miranda Nahmias from MirandaNahmias.com offers a couple of different services on her blog. She offers coaching, done-for-you social media packages, and digital marketing services for clients.

Her January 2018 income report shows that she earned $16,765.05. Of that, $15,900 was from services. You can read all the details of her income and expenses on her blog.

Chapter ten covers providing services in more detail.

ADVERTISING INCOME

You can earn money by allowing advertisements on your blog. Bloggers have several advertising options open to them.

The first is Pay Per Click (PPC). For PPC ads, you earn a small amount each time a reader clicks on the ad. You partner with an ad network and give them space on your site.

Be sure to check with the companies you work with to see how much control you have over the ad content. With some companies, you can select specific industries and have any ads that don't resonate with your audience removed.

Some popular PPC companies are:

> Media.net

> Google AdSense

> Clickbooth

> BlogAds

> Infolinks

If you have decent traffic, you can work directly with companies to sell advertising space. Before approaching a company, you want to have a media kit to share. This includes specific information about your traffic and the demographics of your readers.

Each company has their own set of metrics they're looking for. Often, these include at least 20,000 page views per month.

By comparing your numbers to their metrics, companies can decide if they'd be a good fit for your blog. Once they decide to advertise, you'd put their ad on your site for the agreed upon amount of time.

Another option are Amazon native shopping ads. These allow you to refer shoppers to Amazon. If they make a purchase, you receive a small commission. These are sort of a hybrid between affiliate marketing and ads.

As a beginning blogger, you won't earn a ton of money from ads. There is a definite correlation between traffic and income.

In fact, you may not be eligible to join any advertising networks until you've significantly grown your traffic. Always read the requirements before you apply and make sure you have enough traffic.

If you have enough followers, advertisements can help you earn consistent income from your blog. Mindy, from ThisFairyTaleLife.com, earns money each month from advertising. In her January 2018 monthly income report, she broke down details. She earned $1,876.55 from her blog. Of that, $881.7 was from ad networks. The vast majority of that came from Mediavine.

SPONSORED POSTS

As a blogger, you can partner with brands to create sponsored posts. These are blog posts a company pays you to write. Often your post will need to include a link to a specific product.

Here are some important things to know about sponsored content.

> Don't promote junk. Your readers deserve better.

> Honesty is important. Share your honest opinion, not an over-the-top gushy review.

> You need to disclose the sponsorship, so readers understand the relationship.

> Pick products that align with your blog's niche.

> Offer your readers value even with a sponsored post. Provide a detailed review, compare and contrast products, use a specific ingredient in a simple to prepare recipe. Pick an angle that your readers will find useful.

> Make sure you have a nice mix of sponsored and regular blog posts. You don't want to bombard your readers with sponsored content after sponsored content.

You can find sponsored post opportunities through influencer media networks, by reaching out to brands directly, or through advertising and having brands find you.

Some media networks that work with bloggers are:

> Tapinfluence

> Izea

> She Speaks

> Mom It Forward

You may need to meet certain traffic and social media stats before you qualify to join these networks. The more engaged your audience is, the more value you offer the brand.

If you are interested in doing sponsored posts, make sure you have a media kit with information about your demographics, blog stats, and social media following. This gives brands the information they need to decide whether to work with you.

Your fee per post will play a large part in the amount you can earn. You are bringing value to the brand, so make sure you agree to a fair rate.

Think about how much work the sponsored content will take. Will you need to buy any new photography props or ingredients to create a recipe? These all add to your expenses for the content.

Some bloggers start at $50 for a post, others start at $300. There's no right or wrong answer, just make sure you pick a rate you are comfortable with.

HOSTING EVENTS

The last monetization option is hosting events. Events range from an hour-long webinar to multi-day online summits. In-person conferences, meetups and workshops are other possibilities.

No matter what kind of event you decide to host, make sure you plan it. Don't try to throw something together at the last minute and hope it works.

Test your tech. Make sure everything is operational. And have a tech backup plan, because if something can go wrong, it will.

Write out an agenda. Draft talking points to remind yourself what you should be discussing.

If you involve other people in your event, work closely with them. Put expectations and timelines in writing. Keep everyone in the loop so there are no surprises.

Communicate with your audience as well. Know your pricing structure and put it in writing.

The scope, speakers, and attendance of your event each affect your earning potential. A small one-day meetup with your readers won't bring in as much income as a multi-day virtual summit with influencers in your niche.

There is a ton of potential to earn. Nick Unsworth discusses his experience creating a six-figure virtual summit on the Life on Fire podcast.

START SMALL

There are plenty of ways to monetize your blog. And you want to have multiple streams of income.

But don't dive into everything all at once. If you do, it'll be overwhelming. You may feel like you're in way over your head. Instead, pick one strategy to start with. Once you have that figured out, add another.

Most bloggers start with affiliate marketing. If they are interested in offering a service, they can do this right from the beginning, too.

As they get to know their audience, and understand their pain points, they might create a product. The easiest products to create are digital downloads. You can work your way up to premium video courses, events, and even physical products if those are a good fit for your blog and your audience.

After spending time building up traffic, bloggers might add sponsored posts and advertisements to their monetization plan.

Don't expect to be an overnight success. Every blogger starts at the same place—zero. It takes time, patience, and experience to grow. Don't give up on a monetization strategy after a week or two. Give it time to grow.

ACTION STEPS

1. Write down your income goal for your blog.

2. Review the strategies for monetizing from this chapter. Which ones would be a good fit for your blog and personality?

3. Pick one strategy and begin researching it. Learn more about how other bloggers successfully monetize with that strategy.

4. Start. Put your new knowledge to use and start monetizing your blog.

Phew, we covered a lot of ground in this chapter. Remember to go back and reread this section again down the road. You can't implement everything all at once. In the next chapter, you'll learn specific tips for earning money through affiliate marketing.

CHAPTER EIGHT

Affiliate Marketing

You can't stick affiliate links everywhere and expect money to magically start rolling in. No matter what the "experts" say, it is not a get-rich-quick scheme.

To consistently earn money from affiliate marketing, you must build trust with your audience. It takes time, but it pays off in the long-run.

Since affiliate marketing is a low-cost, low-risk opportunity, many bloggers start here when creating a monetization strategy.

HOW TO BECOME AN AFFILIATE

Unless you are an affiliate with an affiliate link, you aren't going to earn money recommending or reviewing products. If you just stick a standard link to an item on Amazon, or any other company, people can click on it and buy it all day long and you won't see a dime.

You must first become an affiliate for the items or services you want to promote. Often companies or brands run their own affiliate programs. You sign up for these directly on their website. If this is the case, you fill out an online form to apply to become an affiliate. The company will contact you directly to let you know when or if you are approved.

Other companies outsource their affiliate programs to affiliate networks. In this scenario, you join the network and become approved to promote many products. ShareASale is one example. You click on the "Affiliate Sign Up" button on their homepage and create your account. Once approved, you follow a similar process to apply for the different brands. They represent companies like:

> PicMonkey
> Cricut
> Zazzle
> FreshBooks
> Green Kids Crafts

With companies in several different industries, most bloggers find at least a couple of brands that are a good match for their audience.

If you're struggling to find suitable affiliate programs, think about what products or companies you personally use and love. Then type "Name of company + Affiliate program" into Google. Many companies have affiliate programs available, so it's a good idea to check.

UNDERSTAND THE AFFILIATE AGREEMENT

When you become an affiliate for a company, make sure you read the fine print. Before you promote a product through affiliate marketing, make sure you know what the benefit is.

Sometimes you receive a percentage of the sale. Other companies have a flat-rate referral program.

Since companies want to make sure the sale goes through and the product isn't returned, there's often a delay in payment. Some affiliate companies pay out after thirty days, some after seventy-five days or even longer. This information should all be available for you. Become familiar with it.

You also need to be aware of any restrictions or expectations. For instance, Amazon requires you to have their disclosure statement on your blog (see chapter seven).

Terms and conditions get updated occasionally. When they do, read them and look for any major changes. You always need to know what restrictions are in place.

Companies like it when their affiliates are successful, because it means they are selling more. To help you promote their products, many provide you with a variety of tools. In addition to your unique affiliate link, you may find:

> Banners
> Social media images
> Special coupon codes
> Ideas for promotion

> Video instruction to help you earn more as an affiliate

Take time to explore your affiliate dashboard (or portal) and see what is available. If you don't know what you have, you can't use it.

PROVIDE VALUE TO YOUR AUDIENCE

You must earn your audience's trust before they start making purchases you recommend. Part of earning their trust means always providing value.

Don't promote products you don't believe in just because there's a nice affiliate reward. Readers will see through this and quickly walk away.

The following are four tips for always providing value for your readers.

TIP #1: MATCH YOUR NICHE

Are you a fashion blogger? Affiliate links to beauty products, spa services, and idea books for makeup make sense. They fit nicely with your niche and wouldn't seem out of place to your reader.

An affiliate link to a new computer? That connection isn't as obvious. While there may be certain situations where it's appropriate (like if you're posting a behind-the-scenes glimpse at how you blog), your readers won't connect the dots as easily. It will look like you're just in it for the money.

Pick products your ideal reader will benefit from.

TIP #2: DON'T JUST LINK DROP

Stuffing your posts full of affiliate links isn't a good strategy. It overwhelms your reader and cheapens their experience on your blog. Instead, have a purpose behind every link you include.

Are you talking about how you use a specific product each day? Go ahead and include the link. Are you comparing two products? Link to both of them.

For every affiliate link you use, make sure it ties into the content and makes sense.

TIP #3: BE HONEST

No one wants to read a gushing, over-the-top review. There are pros and cons to everything, so many people don't trust that perfect reviews are genuine. Honestly talk about the product. Share what you love, what you like, and what you wish were different. Or share who might really benefit from this product and who probably won't.

This honesty helps your readers learn to value your opinion. It helps them learn to trust you. And if you gain their trust, you will earn a lot more from the products you recommend.

TIP #4: KNOW YOUR READERS

If you want to succeed as an affiliate marketer, you must know your audience. Understand their pain points. Then find products to solve them.

Also, know their budget. If you only recommend big ticket items because that's how you earn the most, you might miss spending from frugal readers.

Back in chapter one, I covered creating your reader avatar. If you haven't done it yet, find time to do it now. You must know who you are selling to, or you won't sell anything.

PROMOTE ON SOCIAL MEDIA

You can include affiliate links in your blog posts, but that's not the only way to promote them. If you disclose, you can share your affiliate links on your social media channels. This includes both your business pages and your personal ones.

Just remember, no one likes the annoying salesperson. Don't let your feeds get bogged down with affiliate links. Instead, include this type of link in your rotation to keep a variety going.

Here are two ideas for wording that don't sound super salesy, and still offer some personal insight or value:

> *My kids love playing with Jenga blocks while I work. They've been building towers, making letters, and creating tunnels for their toy cars. While they play, I get some quiet minutes to knock out a blog post. Win-win! See if your kids love it as much as mine do [insert affiliate link, and disclose by stating this is an affiliate link or by using #afflink].*

Throw a picture in to make it even more personable.

> *Are you thinking of starting a freelance writing career? This course by Gina Horkey was the best investment I made in my business! What do you have to lose? [Insert your affiliate link and disclose.]*

Make sure your content matches the platform. If you're trying to use an affiliate link on Pinterest, make a pin that your readers will click on. On Twitter, use relevant hashtags. On Facebook, tag the company or brand.

And always, always, always disclose that it's an affiliate link.

PROMOTE TO YOUR EMAIL LIST

You can include affiliate links in the emails you send your subscribers. Well, usually. There are exceptions.

Including Amazon affiliate links in your email violates their terms of service. This includes sending out your blog post via RSS feed to your readers. If your readers can click on an affiliate link from your email and wind up on Amazon, you are in violation and risk losing your account.

Other companies may have similar policies. The fine print is important. Ignorance is no excuse. Take time to learn how you can promote your links.

As long as email marketing is permitted, you can include a properly disclosed link or two in your regularly scheduled newsletters.

Just don't let affiliate links take over your emails. No one wants to read that, and your unsubscribe rate will spike.

PROMOTE USING VIDEO

Another idea is to create a video review of the product and include your affiliate link in the comments.

Are you doing a Facebook Live? If you talk about a product in it, include your link in the comments there, too. Remember to disclose.

Video content is shared more frequently; it's a great way to bring more viewers to your content.

PROMOTE WITHIN YOUR PRODUCTS

Are you creating an ebook or a course? If an affiliate product is a good match, include the link.

Of course, you must check the terms and conditions again. This wouldn't work for Amazon links. That's because you can't include Amazon links anywhere but on social media and on your website.

Including links in your products will work for many other affiliate programs. As before, read the fine print so you know what's allowed.

And you can always link to a resource page on your blog, which then provides the Amazon affiliate links for your readers. This is a workaround that many bloggers use.

Even if you aren't creating a product, a resource page is another way to promote affiliate links on your blog.

GO BACK THROUGH YOUR OLD CONTENT

If you wrote any blog posts before you were an affiliate, go back through them. Read your old posts and look for opportunities to update them with your affiliate links.

Perhaps you need to add another paragraph to tie it in. Or add another section to the post.

It's worth taking the time to do, especially on your top-performing posts. Find out which posts are bringing you the most traffic and monetize them.

You really can earn money promoting other people's products. It's a monetization strategy you can start quickly. And it makes a great first step in monetizing your blog.

You can do this. And the feeling when that first deposit makes its way into your account is amazing.

ACTION STEPS

1. Decide whether you want to use affiliate links to monetize your blog or not.

2. Pick 5 to 10 companies to become an affiliate for, and research their affiliate programs (you can add more over time, but this is a good number to start with).

3. Apply to become an affiliate for these companies.

4. Make sure your blog has a disclosure page (see chapter four).

5. Weave an affiliate link into your next blog post.

6. Create a social media update about an affiliate product and include the link (remember to disclose).

7. Go back through your old content and look for ways to include affiliate links.

Affiliate marketing is a great starting point for earning money from your blog. In the next chapter, you'll learn another strategy for monetizing—by offering products that you create.

CHAPTER NINE

Create Your Own Products

You can use your blog as a home base for products you create and services you design. If you need to make money quickly from your blog and already have a following, this is a fabulous starting point. You can use money from your products and services to fund your blogging growth.

The next chapter covers services in more detail. In this chapter, I want to zero in on product creation, which is one of my favorite ways to monetize a blog.

There are two types of products you can sell: digital and physical. Let's look at digital first.

DIGITAL PRODUCTS

Digital products are things that are stored digitally. You don't need to physically mail them to a buyer. Instead, you deliver it via email or provide access online.

There are many possibilities for digital products. Here are six examples:

> Ebooks
> Guides
> Stock photography
> Checklists
> Courses
> Video tutorials

Before you jump into creation mode, do some research. See what people need. What kinds of products will your target audience want to purchase? You want to make sure your product fills a need, or it won't sell. Here are four ways to complete your research:

1. Read the 2-star and 3-star reviews on books in your niche on Amazon. Find out what information readers thought was missing.

2. Head over to Quora.com and see what types of questions relevant to your niche people are asking.

3. Send an email to your subscribers or post a question in a Facebook Group and ask people about their pain points.

4. Create a quick poll for people to take. Facebook, Instagram, and Twitter all support polls.

While researching, you are in information-gathering mode. Get as much data as you can. Then start sifting through it. Look for patterns. Look for gaps in the existing market. See what people want, and consider what you can create to fill that need.

What are your readers' biggest pain points? What problems keep them awake at night? What problems are they willing to pay you to solve?

While analyzing your data, try to answer two main questions.

1. What kind of product am I going to create?

2. What is the big picture topic of this product?

Does your tribe need access to high-quality photographs they can use for commercial purposes? Do they need a beginner's guide to writing web copy?

Are they struggling with time management and wish they had a morning routine checklist to help them stay on track?

Find a need and figure out how to solve it.

CREATE YOUR PRODUCT

Once you know what you want to make, you can begin creating. Start by outlining. Make sure you know exactly what you need to include to get your buyer from point A to point B.

You don't want to promise to solve a problem and then create a product that does something else. Stick to the problem and deliver the solution to your customer.

Some products are quicker to create than others. You might be able to knock out a checklist in a couple of hours. An in-depth, video-based course takes a lot longer, as does an ebook.

To estimate how long your creation stage will take, work backward. Decide how many chapters, lessons, steps, etc., your product will have. Then think about how many you can create in one work session. Be honest here, because you don't want to discourage your progress by thinking you can create it faster than you actually can.

Now you can figure out how many work sessions you need to draft your product. Put the time on your calendar and write down your goal. Share it with someone. Committing publicly to your product creation makes it a lot more real than committing silently.

It may feel strange to tell others about your goals at first, but the accountability is wonderful. Just a simple post on social media works.

Whenever you have extra time, work on your plan. Outline your next chapter. Jot down notes for your videos. Do something every day to make progress on your product.

These baby steps add up. I know from experience, because that's how I created my course, Balancing Diapers and Deadlines.

Once I had it outlined, I found time each day to write content. Some days I knocked out two lessons. Other days, life was crazy, and it was all I could do to outline a single lesson. But by making consistent progress, I got it done.

Don't forgo creating a product just because you don't have a long period to devote to it each day. Baby steps may not race you to the end, but they still get you there.

As you create your product, you might be tempted to keep adding more. I encourage you to be clear about your scope.

Analyze each new idea carefully and see if it's necessary. If it is, add it in. If not, write it down to address in a future product.

Your first product doesn't need to include everything. It just needs to offer a solution to the problem you said you'd solve.

And one last word of warning. In his book, *Finish: Give Yourself the Gift of Done*, Jon Acuff talks about the dangers of perfectionism. The desire to be perfect is what keeps many people from finishing projects. He says:

> *"The harder you try to be perfect, the less likely you'll accomplish your goals."*

Just accept it right now. Your product won't be perfect. Every time you look at it, you will think of something you could improve. So, instead of going for perfection, strive for "good" and "done."

You can always make changes later.

TEST YOUR PRODUCT

Your product won't be perfect, but it should make sense. Get a second set of eyes on it. It's easy for your brain to miss errors since you've been staring at it for so long.

You can enlist some beta testers or hire a professional editor. You could ask a friend to review it in exchange for a couple hours of babysitting.

How you test your product depends on your budget and other resources. But at a minimum, you should get at least one person to review it and provide feedback.

Taking time to test your product will ensure you deliver the best experience for your customers given your available resources. There are many badly compiled digital products on the market today. Don't add to the list.

PACKAGE AND PRICE YOUR PRODUCT

People buy with their eyes. They want to see what they are buying. If your product doesn't look nice, you won't make as many sales. Put some thought into your design.

If you aren't a designer, don't worry. You can use templates in Canva or PicMonkey to create a beautiful cover or image for your product.

Once you've created your product, think about how much you're going to charge for it. Pricing can be complicated. Here are some questions to ask yourself:

1. How much time did you put into creating it?

2. Did you invest any money in the creation of the product? (Editing, design, etc.)

3. At each price point you consider, how many copies would you need to sell to break even?

4. How much flexible income do your readers have?

There's no right or wrong answer when it comes to pricing. You may consider asking a few people what they think it's worth. Pick a starting price and go from there. You can always change it later.

FIGURE OUT YOUR DELIVERY

How are you going to get your product into your buyers' hands? Below are five options for you to consider, depending on the type of product you sell and the resources you have available.

OPTION #1: THIRD-PARTY SERVICE

If you're selling a downloadable product, such as an ebook, a guide, or a checklist, you can use a third-party service to sell. These are free (or paid) accounts you sign up for.

You can upload your file and integrate it to your site with a "Buy Now" button. When a buyer clicks on it, they are sent to the third-party site to complete payment. That site digitally delivers the product.

Here are four services you can compare:

> Easy Digital Downloads (free starter plan)
> Podia (allows you to offer both downloads and courses for $39/month)
> SendOwl (what I currently use, $15/month starter plan)
> Gumroad ($10/month starter plan)

Take some time to read the terms and conditions of each. See which plan will work best for your needs.

OPTION #2: STORE PLUG-IN ON YOUR WEBSITE

Another option for selling goods is to turn your website into an ecommerce site through a WordPress plugin.

This keeps you in control of the whole process from start to finish. However, this requires more technical know-how to ensure you integrate multiple components (like a way to get paid and required plugins) correctly.

You can set up your store to automatically deliver digital products after purchase. If you are personally shipping a physical product, you can see the orders as they come in.

One downside of turning your site into an ecommerce site is the increased security you must provide. You need to ensure your customers have a safe and secure connection for payment.

If you'd like to explore this possibility, here are three plugins you can compare:

> WooCommerce (free)

> eCommerce Shopping Cart by WP Easy Cart (free plugin to install, but requires a $50 license to use)

> Cart66 ($9.99/month after a free trial)

If you decide to go this route, make sure your site meets the legal requirements for e-commerce.

OPTION #3: AN EMAIL COURSE

Some courses work well for delivery via email, especially if they are text based. One possibility is to drip the content out to your readers. When you drip content, you send out one lesson each day or each week over a scheduled period.

If you don't want your readers to have to wait for the next lesson, you can set up your course on demand. After finishing one lesson, your reader clicks on a button and the next lesson is automatically sent.

The process of setting up this delivery is beyond the scope of this book. There are plenty of YouTube videos detailing the process for the main Email Service Providers.

OPTION #4: A COURSE HOSTED ON YOUR SITE

If you want your students to log into a system to access online course materials, you can install courseware on a subdomain of your site.

On my subdomain, students can access my free and paid courses. It looks different than my main site, because it's running the theme recommended by the Zippy Courses plugin I use to create the courses.

Your host company should help you create a subdomain. These are free with most companies, but be sure to verify this. You don't want to wind up with unexpected charges.

Once you have your subdomain, treat it like a brand new site. Install WordPress and the plugins you need for your course.

You can also run a courseware plugin on your main site, but you risk running into compatibility issues with your theme and other plugins.

Here are three plugins you can consider for courseware:

> Zippy Courses Plugin

> LearnPress

> LearnDash

OPTION #5: A COURSE HOSTED VIA A THIRD-PARTY

Many bloggers don't want to deal with the technical burden of self-hosting their course and integrating with a payment processor. Instead, they opt to use a third-party system.

Here are four platforms for hosting courses:

1. Teachable

2. Podia

3. Udemy

4. Ruzuku

Make sure to read the details of your agreement no matter which platform or plugin you use. Find out if you need to pay a percentage of your sales, a flat annual fee, or a one-time fee.

PROMOTE YOUR PRODUCT

You can't just create a product and expect sales to happen. You must market.

Schedule social media blasts. Try to write guest posts on influencers' sites and mention your product in your bio. Weave it into your blog posts. Send a special coupon out to your list.

If you get good feedback from a student, ask for permission to use their words as a testimonial. This social proof will help you in your promotions.

Keep promoting your product throughout the coming months. You can't just tell your people once and then forget about it.

ACTION STEPS

1. Decide if you want to offer a product.
2. Pick one type of product to begin with.
3. Follow the steps in this chapter to work through creating your product.

In the next chapter, I will dive into services. Offering a one-on-one service is the fastest way to earn money from your blog. You only need a handful of customers to make your first four figures from home.

CHAPTER TEN

Offering Services

When you offer services, you are trading your skills for money. There are plenty of opportunities available. Pick a single service to start. After you go through the process once, it's easier to add more services in the future. But if you try to do too much at once, you risk confusing your potential clients and you can become overwhelmed quickly.

PICK YOUR SERVICE

I shared a list of ten services back in chapter seven. These are just the beginning of the possibilities. There are many services you can offer.

If you are having trouble deciding, think about what your friends and family always ask you to help with. Are you their go-to proofreader? Or the person they call when they have technical difficulties?

Pick something you enjoy doing because it's a lot harder to keep at something you hate, even if it pays well.

Avoid becoming a generalist. Specialists earn a lot more money. If you are a freelance writer, what sorts of topics do you want to be known as an expert in? If you are a coach, what are your specialties? You can't coach everyone, so where are you going to shine?

In addition to niching down your services, you will want to niche down your ideal clients. Do you want to offer VA services to people who run tech companies? Or do you want to offer blog management services to busy mompreneurs?

Take time to think through this process. Just like picking a niche for your blog, you can always pivot if what you select first isn't working.

HOW MUCH SHOULD YOU CHARGE?

Rates for services vary greatly. Remember, you will have to pay taxes on any income you earn. Plan on setting aside at least 25 percent. Keep this in mind as you determine your rate. If you're charging $15/hour, you only get to keep $11.25 of that. Is $11.25 an hour worth your time?

Only you can decide that. When I started as a virtual assistant, my starting rate was $30/hour. After I took out a quarter for taxes, it was a rate I felt comfortable with as a beginner.

In this article, Sally suggests some starting rates for popular freelancing services: www.sallyannmiller.com/first-1k-from-home/

She also advises that you start on the lower end. Then, after you attract your first few paying gigs, gradually increase your rates. But don't start too low. Bargain hunters are often the worst clients.

MOVING AWAY FROM THE HOURLY RATE

Do you know the downside of charging hourly? There are two, actually.

The first is you have to keep track of your time. When you're a busy mom, you might have five minutes to work here, ten minutes to work there. Adding up all those small chunks isn't as easy as it sounds!

Now for the big problem: You get penalized for being an expert. Think about it. The better you get at your job, the quicker you become. But when you do the job more quickly, you get paid less. Less pay for the same amount of work isn't a good deal for you.

To combat this, consider moving away from hourly rates. Instead, charge by the product or package. Your client will know what to expect, and so will you. It's a great way to build up some recurring income.

CREATE HIRE ME AND CONTACT PAGES

Once you pick a service, create a new page on your blog. This can be called "Hire Me" or "Work with Me" or something similar.

On this page, detail the services you offer. If applicable, include samples. For instance, on my Hire Me page for writing, I link to some of my best articles.

You will also want to include testimonials on this page. Social proof is important, and it makes you look more professional.

Some people include their pricing on their website, others choose not to. There's no right or wrong there. Do what you feel is best.

Lastly, provide a way for potential clients to get in touch. I use a standard contact form. Other people have potential buyers schedule a discovery call.

ADVERTISE YOUR SERVICE

Let people know you're starting to offer a new service. Send a shout-out on your social media channels. Email and call people you know. Your existing network already knows you. They are more likely to hire you or refer you to someone they know looking for the services you offer.

If you're in any Facebook groups that offer a promotion day, you can include a link to your new page. You need to get the word out so that people know you are available for hire.

Bonus Tip: Always frame your service in terms of the benefit to your client. What outcome or result do you provide? For example, if you offer virtual assistant services, you can ask: *"Do you know anyone who needs xyz tasks taken off their plate, so they can focus on growing their business?"*

WHERE TO FIND GIGS

People probably won't find you at the very beginning. You must go find them. You can look for gigs:
> On job boards
> Within Facebook groups
> By asking people in your personal network

> By cold-pitching your ideal clients

Once you find a job, make sure you get the details in writing. You can use a contract to help protect both parties.

Do your best work on every assignment. Meet the deadline and exceed your client's expectations. Your reputation is essential to your service offerings. Do your best to make it a good one.

ACTION STEPS

1. Decide if you want to offer a service.
2. Pick one service to start with.
3. Follow the steps in this chapter to create your "Hire Me" page.

You now have the information you need to earn consistently from your blog!

There's only one more topic to cover. In the final chapter, I will show you how to juggle your time so you can grow a blog while raising a family.

CHAPTER ELEVEN

Find Time to Blog

Finding time to get it all done is a challenge, especially if you're a busy mom. And if you're going to create a successful, money-making blog, you must add time to blog into your day. It will take time to find a routine that works for you. It's worth the effort, because you will be working from home doing something you love. As your blog grows, you will build a steady income from your home, with your kids by your side.

As a homeschooling mom of eight children, I've discovered five key principles to making time to blog. These principles didn't happen instantly. They all come from lessons learned the hard way.

You might have to think creatively to figure out what works for your family. The strategies I use may not work for you, but don't give up.

I'm a huge fan of looking for bottlenecks in my day. When I notice we keep struggling with the same thing repeatedly, I look for solutions. Necessity really is the mother of invention.

For instance, when I first started freelance writing, I struggled to find time. It seemed whenever I sat down to write, my kids would all need me simultaneously. They'd whine and cry and fight, and I'd get frustrated.

I got tired of staying up late trying to work when they were in bed, so I started brainstorming. My mom taught kindergarten for years, and she always had "Quiet Work Time" in her classroom after lunch recess. This calmed the kids back down before jumping into the afternoon learning.

I knew there had to be a way to modify this idea for my family. One day, when I needed a little extra time to work, I asked everyone to bring down some paper and crayons. I got the baby situated in a booster seat at the table with some board books while everyone else found a spot around the room.

I set the timer for fifteen minutes and instructed everyone to create something they could show off when the timer beeped. The first day was a little rough, and required *lots* of redirecting. But I didn't give up. We kept trying.

After a week or two, Family Writing Time had become a routine. The older kids model the behavior for the little ones, and everyone loves sharing time at the end. We added a few minutes each week, and now everyone can sit and quietly work on a project of choice for thirty minutes. The older kids could go longer, but I'd lose the little ones. We decided to stick with this length.

Family Writing Time isn't the only way I find time to blog, but it's one of my kids' favorites. Here's an overview of the five strategies I use daily to find time for blogging.

STRATEGY #1: MINIMIZE YOUR DECISIONS

Your brain can only handle so much before it gets overloaded. If you're constantly stopping to make small decisions, you won't be as productive. To help keep your brain from experiencing decision fatigue, make as many decisions beforehand as you can. Here are three specific ways I've minimized my decisions.

1. Meal Planning

I used to spend a lot of time figuring out what we were going to eat each day. The kids asked about food so many times every day:

"Mom, what's for breakfast?"

"Mom, what's for lunch?"

"Mom, what's for dinner?"

Since I didn't know, I had to stop what I was doing and think about it. Sometimes I even rummaged through the cupboards to try to figure it out.

Then I created the annual meal plan. It's been life changing. Now the kids know what's for breakfast, lunch, dinner, and snack every day of the week. They no longer ask me. And I haven't rummaged through the cupboard in a long time.

An annual meal plan might not work for your family, but I encourage you to find a meal planning system that fits your needs and stick to it. The time saved is incredible.

2. Cleaning Schedule

Each July when we customize our annual meal plan, we review our cleaning schedule and assign new chores. This helps keep the house running on autopilot. I don't have to stop and decide who needs to unload the dishwasher this week, or whose turn it is to take out the trash. Everyone knows.

When it's time, I can say, "Remember to do your chores," and everyone knows what to do. By keeping the same chores for a year, my kids become experts at them. This cuts down the amount of time I need to spend checking their work.

When we complete our afternoon chores, we spend a little extra time on one area of the house each day. This gives us dedicated time to tackle some of the deep cleaning tasks.

Our house isn't spotless, but this system helps it stay presentable. And I'm no longer trying to keep track of cleaning tasks in my head, or trying to remember what we need to do or when.

3. Give the Kids a Day

A couple of years ago, I assigned each of my kids a day. On their assigned day, each child can:

> Pick the bedtime story

> Select the TV show to watch during dinner prep

> Lick the spoon if I bake

> Pick who they sit next to during meals

> Be my helper if I need small tasks done

And no one complains, because they get to do the same thing on their day. Knowing I have one child each day to make many of the small decisions helps me tremendously.

4. Decide in Advance When You Will Work

You must make blogging a habit. To help make that happen, decide in advance when you will work on your blog. You might get up an hour early, or work after you drop the kids off at school. Find time periods that work for you and put it on your calendar. Set a reminder on your phone if that helps you remember.

Otherwise, you may not think about it. Especially at first. Since it's a new endeavor for you, you must be proactive in making yourself remember to work on it. For more ideas on when to work, see strategy five below.

STRATEGY #2: CUT TASKS FROM YOUR PLATE

It's time for a hard truth. You can't do it all. At least, you can't do it all perfectly. If your schedule is already full, making time to blog means you need to cut something out. Or you need to decide to lower your expectations for some of your tasks.

Proactively making these decisions now will save you from feeling like you're a failure or simply feeling overwhelmed. You aren't dropping tasks, you are purposefully deciding to remove them. It's a slight difference, but a powerful one.

Look for tasks you can cut completely or change to take less time. You might watch less TV, drop the weekly story-time outing, or buy bread instead of making it.

Think about everything on your plate and pick your priorities. Review your schedule a couple of times a year. Life constantly changes. Make sure your priorities are still a match for your current season.

STRATEGY #3: USE SMALL BITS OF TIME THAT WERE OTHERWISE UNACCOUNTED FOR

My days are full of tiny chunks of time. It's important to have a plan for those minutes, or else they're wasted. There are many blogging tasks you can do in five minutes. Here are ten:

1. Schedule some social media posts.
2. Leave a comment on some blog posts in your niche.
3. Brainstorm headline ideas.
4. Find a creative commons photo to use in your next Pin.
5. Create a new cover image for your blog post with a template.
6. Test some headlines in the Headline Analyzer.
7. Brainstorm a freebie you could make.
8. Start outlining a post.
9. Think through the topic you're writing about and jot down any ideas you have.
10. Check your comments: deal with any spam and respond to real ones.

Create a list of small tasks. When you have five or ten minutes, you won't have to waste any time trying to decide what to do.

These small chunks of time add up. If you can find six five-minute periods throughout the day, you just dedicated thirty minutes to your blog. That's 2.5 hours after five days.

STRATEGY #4: ACCEPT HELP

What can you let other people help you with? When I started blogging, my kids helped more in the cooking and cleaning departments. They're learning important skills, and I have more time.

My spouse has also helped out. For instance, he often tackles my table chores after dinner. This gives me a few extra minutes of work time.

If I have a tight deadline approaching, I occasionally ask my parents to take a couple of the kids. They enjoy spending time together, and it really helps.

I also let my kids help me work. They've taken pictures, created pins, proofread posts, and more. Kids can do more than many people give them credit for.

I used to think asking for help meant I was a failure. I wanted to do everything. But all that did was wear me down. There's no such thing as Supermom. Cut yourself some slack. The world isn't going to end because you weren't the one to cook dinner or clean the toilet.

STRATEGY #5: FIND MULTIPLE WORK PERIODS

When you are juggling kids and blogging, it's a lot harder to create a strict schedule. Life happens and so do interruptions. So, you need a flexible plan.

I've discovered the importance of picking four different work periods during the day. When life is crazy, and I miss one or two, I still have opportunities to use the other ones.

Here's my current plan for carving blogging time into my day.

1. Early Mornings

I enjoy the early mornings because it's one of the few times my house is quiet. It's a good time to focus on writing before the kids wake up. But getting up early is definitely easier during some seasons of life than others. When I'm up with the kids at night, I opt for sleep in the mornings instead of word counts.

2. Family Writing Time

Each weekday, we spend thirty minutes on Family Writing Time. During this time, I write. My kids sit quietly and work independently on a task. They might:

> Color pictures

> Do crafts

> Write a story

> Draw characters from a book they read

> Create stories from game pieces (Memory, Tell Me a Story, and Morphology Jr. are current favorites)

> Write a poem

> Practice their cursive

> Cut letters out of a newspaper

> Stack up letter blocks

> Play with our foam letter puzzle

They just need to work quietly and not disrupt anyone else. When our timer beeps, we clean up. Then we take turns sharing what we did. It's a fun way to spend time with my kids while working on my blog.

3. Quiet Time

Once my kids turn three, they start fighting naps. But I didn't want to give up that long work time, so we transitioned to quiet time. For ninety minutes each afternoon, my youngest kids nap. While they sleep, the rest of the house has quiet time.

The kids each select an activity and a space and play independently during this time. Quiet time goes most smoothly when we create a schedule. This keeps the kids rotating through activities. Here are ten of my kids' favorites:

1. Working on a jigsaw puzzle

2. Doing an art project

3. Sewing

4. Writing

5. Using pattern blocks and a book of patterns

6. Train tracks

7. Building blocks

8. Baby dolls and the toy kitchen

9. Doing dress up

10. Playing with playdough

While the kids have quiet time, I get to work. This is when I do a lot of my blog post writing. The key here is having the kids engaged while I work. If I just turn them loose without a plan, I probably won't like the choices they make. That's when I end up with crazy messes to clean.

By spending a few minutes to plan and get the kids settled, I'm able to get more done.

4. Evenings

I'm not a night owl. By about nine o'clock, my brain starts shutting down. Which means when I try to stay up late to write, it takes me longer than it should. And the quality is never as good.

To combat this, my husband and I put our kids to bed early. By 7:30, everyone but our teenager is tucked in. This way, I can write for an hour in the evenings before it's time for me to call it quits.

And since we moved their bedtime up, my kids are getting enough sleep. As a result, they whine a lot less during the day.

DO WHAT WORKS FOR YOU

When you are trying to find time to blog, you must do what works for you and your family. If you work best late at night, stay up later. If your kids are in school, work during midday.

Keep trying different strategies. If one doesn't work, don't give up completely. It doesn't mean you weren't meant to blog; it just means you haven't found the strategy that works for you and your family yet. Keep experimenting and brainstorming.

PRIORITIZE EACH DAY

At the start of each day, make time to look at what you need to do for your blog. Then, prioritize your list. Decide what to focus on first.

This stops you from getting sidetracked by tasks that aren't as important. You only have so much time to work on your blog. You need to focus on tasks that attract income and build an audience.

If a daily prioritizing session doesn't fit your schedule, try doing it weekly. Is there time you can spend each Sunday going over the upcoming week and prioritizing everything you want to get done?

It doesn't matter what your prioritizing time looks like. All that matters is that you look at everything on your plate and decide where to dedicate your attention and energy.

Consistent baby steps pay off. Make it a point to work on your blog each day and do something to manage your monetization plan.

ACTION STEPS

1. Think about your current schedule. When can you fit in time for blogging?

2. Make a list of tasks you can accomplish in 5 to 10 minutes. Whenever you have spare time, get in the habit of doing something from this list.

3. Make a list of activities to engage your kids while you work.

4. Commit to doing something every day to help grow your blog.

CHAPTER TWELVE

Now What?

Now that you understand what it takes to build a money-making blog, it's time to build yours. Whether you want to earn a full-time income from home, or bring in a little side-money each month, blogging can help. You can earn money from blogging, even as a busy stay-at-home mom.

> *You won't earn money from a blog that only exists in your mind. You must take action.*

The chapters in this book show you how to set up your blog, get it ready for readers, and create sharable content. You have what you need to start. Once you start, it gets easier. Remember, you only have to write your first blog post once.

Don't stop with that first post. Keep writing. Keep marketing. Keep monetizing. Find what works for you, and keep doing it. If you need extra help, be sure to check out the bonus area at sallyannmiller.com/bloggingbook. Sally and I packed it full of goodies to help you succeed.

> *Your ideal readers need to hear from you. Your voice is missing in your niche.*

Launch your blog and start sharing the content your readers want. The world is ready for your voice—so what are you waiting for?

ABOUT SALLY MILLER

Sally is a mom on a mission. She is passionate about answering the question, "Can modern moms have it all?" In a previous life, Sally worked for nineteen years as a project manager and business analyst in London and Silicon Valley. She has a Bachelor's Degree in Computer Science and a Master's Degree in Business Administration.

When her daughter was born, she discovered a new purpose. Sally left her corporate career to be a stay-at-home mom. She wanted to be a full-time mom to her kids. However, she missed the freedom and purpose that came from working. So Sally made a decision: She'd find a way to stay home with her kids and earn an income (without feeling torn between the two).

Sally is a self-confessed research geek and compulsive planner. She loves learning how stuff works, mastering new skills, and sharing her knowledge with others. Since leaving her nine-to-five, Sally has published six books (and counting). She's also started multiple businesses and is committed to helping others like her earn an income from home.

You can find out more by visiting her website at sallyannmiller.com.

ABOUT LISA TANNER

Lisa is a homeschooling mom to eight kids, ranging from teen to tot. She's also a freelance writer, virtual assistant, and blogger.

But, owning a business hasn't always been Lisa's goal. When she was younger, the only thing she planned to do was teach. She earned her master's degree in elementary reading and literacy, and taught for seven years in the public schools of Washington. Then, the time was right for her to come home and teach her own children.

Lisa loves animals and enjoys life on the family farm. She and her family spend evenings playing board games, kicking a soccer ball around, and just hanging out together. They also enjoy loading up the little family school bus and exploring the backroads of beautiful eastern Washington.

Lisa enjoys helping busy moms tame the chaos in their lives and find success in whatever they decide to do. You can find out more about Lisa and discover her tips for balancing diapers and deadlines by visiting her website: lisatannerwriting.com.

32933947R00073

Made in the USA
Middletown, DE
10 January 2019